"The explosive popularity of virtual worlds like Second Life and World of Warcraft has thrown a bright cultural spotlight on the avatar—the ephemeral body that represents us in these worlds—but nothing has illuminated it quite like Mark Stephen Meadows' *I, Avatar*. Deeply thoughtful, and vibrantly informed by Meadows' lived encounters with virtual worlds, the book makes a compelling case for extending the concept of the avatar beyond the boundaries of those worlds, across the full range of digitally mediated experience, and into the core of what makes us human."
—Julian Dibbell, author of *Play Money: Or How I Quit My Day Job and Made Millions Trading Virtual Loot*

"Mark Meadows explores and explains one of the most intriguing phenomena of digital life: the fantastic (psychological) reproduction of a self who inhabits a range of virtual worlds. He narrates how our avatars/ourselves have co-evolved with the development of new virtual worlds, revealing new modes of human-becoming in a digital age."
—Anne Balsamo, Author, *Designing Culture: The technological Imagination at Work* and Professor, Interactive Media at USC

"Mark Meadows is fully immersed in an evolving new culture and reporting back from the heart of the action. Ultimately, what he reports on isn't informing us about Second Life, World of Warcraft, or online chat rooms. Instead, what he reveals is a reflection of ourselves a the beginning of the 21st Century in all our weirdness, wonder, and humanity."
—Nathan Shedroff, Experience Strategist

"What Bruce Chatwin did for the exotic far reaches of the physical world, Mark Stephen Meadows does for the virtual. *I, Avatar* is a richly informed and intensely personal set of travel dispatches from the thriving frontier that is Second Life. The author/artist's picaresque narrative records his journey through the construction of his online persona "pighed" as well as the shifting social contexts in differing online communities. The result is a thought-provoking and illuminating exploration of the social and philosophical underpinnings of perceived realities both physical and virtual."
—Maribeth Back, Senior Research Scientist, FX-PAL

"In this sweeping and impressive work, Mark Meadows traces the history of online avatars and explores the profound roles that they play in our online lives by mediating our communication with others and contributing to our social interactions, activities, and group narratives. The work is thus not just about avatars, but ultimately about the strategies that humans use to present themselves when they communicate, work together, and play together. It will be an invaluable resource for disciplines ranging from virtual world design to narrative theory to sociology."
—Peter Ludlow, Professor of philosophy, University of Toronto, and co-author of *The Second Life Herald*

"Mark Meadows' virtual creatures are not your next door neighbours—or are they? Leaving behind 1990s cyberculture and its underground aesthetics, with Meadows we descend into a maelstrom of Identity 2.0 in which business, leasure, sexuality, labour and fashion melt into one."
—Geert Lovink, Media Theorist, Net Critic, and Activist

"I knew Mark Meadows was a weird mix: smart, adventurous, well-read, well-spoken, nerdy, but most of all open minded. He has managed to work all this into his book. That should tell you what kind of a trip this read is. If anyone was to bring something fresh to the table, it had to be Mark Meadows."
—Alexis Nolent, Ubisoft's Game System Story Director
and author of world-famous graphic novel *The Killer.*

"As anyone who has heard Mark Meadows speak on portraiture, interactivity and narrative knows, he connects with the imagination and intellect of his audience in a way that is both thrilling and artistic. Little wonder then that his new book, *I, Avatar,* connects with the reader in much the same way."
—Matt Costello, Co-creator of ZoogDisney and Writer of
Doom 3 and The 7th Guest

"Pighed takes us on a whirlwind road trip through this century's most exciting new medium, the exploding cyber-suburbs of virtual worlds inhabited by millions of avatars. Do you want to know how your avatar reflects back on you? Are you asking the question: where will this strange journey take us? Don't just stand there, the front seat is free, so get yourself strapped in for upload!"
—Bruce Damer, Virtual Worlds Pioneer and Author of *Avatars*

"Avatars are fast becoming the main vehicle through which we navigate an ever more complex online landscape. Mark documents with vivid imagery the blurring line between our real and virtual identities, the multi-faceted ways in which we project ourselves into bodies ranging from a simple string of text to furry, phantasmagoric creatures. A recommended read to anyone interested in the current and future culture of cyberspace."
—Nicolas Ducheneaut, Researcher, Xerox-PARC

"Gorgeously illustrated by both imagery and personal recollections, *I, Avatar* is a whimsical, well-informed introduction to the virtual world experience and its broader implications by a seasoned guide with valuable secrets to impart."
—Wagner James Au, author of *The Making of Second Life*

I, AVATAR:
The Culture and Consequences of Having a Second Life

❦ ❦

Mark Stephen Meadows

I, Avatar: The Culture and Consequences of Having a Second Life
Mark Stephen Meadows

New Riders
1249 Eighth Street
Berkeley, CA 94710
510/524-2178
510/524-2221 (fax)

Find us on the Web at: www.newriders.com
To report errors, please send a note to errata@peachpit.com

New Riders is an imprint of Peachpit, a division of Pearson Education

Project Editor: Becky Morgan
Production Editor: David Van Ness
Copyeditor: Corbin Collins
Indexer: FireCrystal Communications

Design, Portrait Photographs, and Cover Design: Mark Stephen Meadows / pighed
Cover Photograph: Amélie Padioleau

ISBN 13: 978-0-321-53339-5
ISBN 10: 0-321-53339-9

9 8 7 6 5 4 3 2 1

Printed and bound in the United States of America

CONTENTS

"Following the light of the sun, we left the Old World."
—Christopher Columbus
"Isles of the Blessed"

The Strange Migration

A strange migration is occurring, and it deserves to be documented.

The migration is headed into a kind of "Wild West," a "new world," one marked by massive automation, promises of wealth, rampant lawlessness, rumors of ruination, emerging cults, political upheaval, moral lasciviousness, and questions about what impact these things will create in the coming years. The migration verges on a stampede. Its destination is a strange land where settlers from all over the world dress in outlandish costumes. The linguistic landscape is composed of English, but 34 percent of the inhabitants are European, with a growing number of Asians and those from elsewhere. The fastest growing city of its kind, the population has doubled, at times, in only months. And the immigrants are young, with over 70 percent of the population between the ages of 18 and 34. Ranking fifth among the cities in the United States and fourth among metropolitan areas, this "promised land" is about to become a major international center, like New York or Paris. Forty-four percent of the population is female—up from just a year ago and headed towards a more natural balance. Sun-bronzed, broad-shouldered, rock-jawed Adonises walk the landscape, people who appear to be in perfect health—virile, fertile Greek gods who have just descended from a nearby Olympus.

This is an exotic landscape where the climate is comfortable and the sky is not cloudy all day. Extreme speculation is driving property to appreciate at over 100 percent or more in a single year. Vast estates are bought and then divided, usually the week after purchase, into smaller subsections for resale to the highest bidders, who then redivide again and resell. The immigrants have built not so much a city as a series of connecting villages. Taxes are often non-existent. Manufacturing costs are low. Profit margins are high. The borders to this development area are growing quickly, expanding at more than twice the predicted rate.

The automated, subdivided, speedy-turnaround approach to real estate is reflected in what is built. Construction is cheap, fast, and dirty. Houses are erected in multiples, each one precisely like the other, subdivided sprawls that can be bought pre-stocked, with just about everything included (glassware, dishes, landscaping, furniture, and so on). Many of the buildings are designed to look like "the old country," to give a sense of familiarity and continue the customs of the well-known homeland. Much of the real estate has been managed by a female real estate mogul who is referred to by first name only and is famous for starting from nothing and amassing a fortune on what few saw coming.

It is a world driven by the people that drive the media, a world of the screen, of narrative, of simulation and imitation in art. Unknown citizens become international celebrities overnight, their images broadcast to millions of screens around the world. The very fact that it is a city founded on media is what has helped it to grow, generating great hype and an intoxicating promise of fame, leisure, and fortune. The image of beautiful people walking hand in hand, is broadcast far and wide, enticing people to come to this new world where their imagination is the only thing that limits their potential.

This world is Los Angeles, 1929, just a few years before the Great Depression. In the decades that followed, the city and the surrounding southern California region would become dominated by automobiles, McDonald's, Disneyland—becoming a land of profitable automation, easy luxury, inexpensive fun, and independence.

This is also the world of Second Life as it was in 2006, the virtual online world also dedicated to profitable automation, easy luxury, inexpensive fun, and independence. Itself a product of the American Dream, Second Life produces hordes of Kens and Barbies we call *avatars*. Like vehicles driven through an online landscape, they float blank-eyed in their magic kingdom, each hoping to strike it rich, become a star, find a friend, or simply explore new possibilities. It is just like 1920s L.A., where strange media hype and the lure of a "new world" attract immigrants from everywhere.

The dreams of Los Angeles and Second Life are similar; both say you can be someone else by simply setting foot there. And to some degree, they are right.

The immigrants coming to Second Life and other avatar systems are armed with ambitions to sell temptations. Some are here to solve problems that can't be solved in their "first" life, and some are here to make new lives. All are here to make their dreams as real as possible—to deal these dreams out like cards on a table and play them against the other immigrants in this brave new world.

I've lived for more than two years in both Los Angeles and Second Life.

What follows is an account of what I've found in my travels as an avatar. I discovered a city of strange people intent on creating real dreams. I encountered a virtual slave pursued by real traders, and a real slave playing with virtual traders. I struggled with the impact of the virtual on the real and found out how the psychological line between them becomes hazy and thin and can be crossed as easily as logging into a website.

Most of all I found the avatar to be a machine that is attached to the psychology of its user. From within that machine the driver can peek out, squinting through alien eyes, and find a new world. And, oddly, the driver can also look into himself, as if gazing into his navel, and find a new landscape inside as well.

My first avatar was a string of six letters. I mostly used it to make friends and abuse strangers.

In the fall of 1993 I traded a painting for a modem. It arrived in the mail in a cardboard box, couched in marketing and manuals, about as complicated as an FM radio, and included giveaway software. Part of that software was a subscription to America Online. I popped in the floppy disk and was asked for my screen name.

On a moment's inspiration I typed in PigHed. A friend that day had called me pigheaded, which I am, and pigs have always attracted me because they seem been both horrific and adorable, and I suppose that *Lord of The Flies* had something to do with it, too. I would have typed in Pig Head, but the system only allowed six characters, so I typed in what I did and, having set a sign on my shiny new virtual forehead, I set out to explore.

AOL's architecture was chatroom based. The interface consisted of boxes with text in them that were organized so that groups could form around particular discussion topics. These chatrooms had names like *Anonymous and Gay* or *Auto Shop* so that you would be able to click in and meet people who were gay and anonymous or into fixing 'trannies. For a day or two it seemed that the population was mostly computer repair technicians with hobbies. Though the architecture was set up to group people, I didn't find much that interested me.

Looking at the list of names of people that were online, I saw names like Ppaul, Deb4d, blatsky, Mandus, MikeP, and someone named Swine.

Swine. A like-minded porker?

I sent him a message that said, "Nk, nk."

A message came back. "Grnt, Grnt."

A month later our little group had grown, thanks to a few equally inarticulate messages, to include people with names like P0rc, Pigg, Bakon, and Piggy. We burned time in a flagrant fashion, typing ham-headed jokes to one another and pushing the boundaries of porcine humor.

```
Pigg > I'm going to hock my hams over in "Singles Chat" today.
Orc > You selling tenderloin or sausage?
Piggy > I'll see your sausage and braise you one!!
Bakon > Don't leave me out, I've got some fatback to sell.
```

Most of this content was juvenile, because, well, most of us in the group were juvenile. We roamed around, nomadic and marauding. We'd appear in some chatroom containing three or four hapless chatters and we'd start discussing pork products. Specifically Spam.

```
Bakon > May the Spam be with you!
Piggy > This little spammy went to market,
Pigg >          And with you as well, Bakon.
Piggy > this little spammy stayed home,
ill433 > Will you guys knock it off, please?
Piggy > this little spammy had spam-beef,
Piggy > and this little spammer had none!
Orc > Knock off the spam!
Pigg > and this little spammer cried WEE WEE WEE ALL THE SPAM H
ill433 > That does it, I'm outta here..
```

The conversation was intended to annoy to such a degree that no one else could participate. We ended up spending most of our time, as the weeks went by, in The Kitchen, or Raiding The Fridge—chatrooms devoted to food. We devoted our energies to heckling people and seeing how many people we could piss off, and how quickly. We relied on the canned pork product known as Spam. We were the scourge of the system. It was our goal.

To tell the truth, we didn't talk about a lot more than Spam, and several of us got our accounts canceled. But what we were doing was more than simple hostility to the docile system and its contributors. Years later I realized that there was an unwritten list of rules our little band of piggies had followed. The first rule was the name. In order to be part of our herd you had to have a name that had something to do with pigs or pig-based products. The second rule was that you had to be willing to descend into the murky and absurd with puns around this theme, passing time typing with American juveniles who were probably as busy dripping pizza grease on their shirt as they were adjusting headphones. And third, you had to be willing to pointlessly harangue other people who were not part of the band of boorish boars.

Without being aware of what we'd done, we had formed a small group that, just like Anonymous and Gay or Auto Shop, allowed us to share information that was valuable to each member of the group. Rather than look for common interests in the names of chatroom, we did it by using the names of our characters. We did it in a way that AOL had not, probably, imagined at the time. We did it by our names that we provided, rather than by the architecture that AOL provided. The AOL architecture was there to group and separate people, which was ultimately what we used our names for. It's just that the "community" we'd made, our profiles, our friends, our jokes, our group, and our entire reason for being together, were all based on our names—our avatars.

These days nearly a fifth of the planet's population uses similar systems to socially spend time. According to Nielsen NetRatings, general community, preceded only by search engines and email, is the third most-used application of the Internet. Offline or online, social interfaces still work largely the same way. People find one another based on similar interests, common friends, or like names. Only now we have a picture to go with it.

PROFILE: YOUR VITAL STATISTICS
FRIENDS: YOUR IMMEDIATE SOCIETY
GROUPS: YOUR DISTANT SOCIETY

Twelve very geeky months later I logged onto a BBS in Sausalito, California named The WELL. The WELL went online in February of 1985 and accepted its first paying customer two months later. It quickly grew to be known as a community that did things together in real life—weddings, funerals BBQs, and so forth. By 1993 it had a staff of 12 and more than 7,000 users, and I was invited to work there as a graphic designer to build its website's front end, the third on the Internet.

I registered my username as Pighed again and, as I had done in America Online, I began to look for other people in this new world. It was a bit like AOL in that there were topics, or rooms, that people could visit, but it felt different because the level of conversation demanded some thought. I imagined it a bit like a forest, with glades and fields where people would sit and talk, and with technical cliffs that I still had to climb. Sometimes I would notice names I'd seen before, and people I thought of as locals, Gail or Howard or Jonl or Bruce. These seemed like people using their given names, or a slight variation. Occasionally I would see more fantastic creatures like Loompanx, Vision, or Wolfy.

I wandered the woods of The WELL and met people, or their avatars, or something that was a person, but not. I met Paco, Monte, Sulfuric, and Magdalen. Magdalen was not only a resident of this online world, she was also an employee of The WELL and sat right next to Sulfuric. Her given name was Tiffany. Sulfuric's was David. And when I met Tiffany she called me Pighed and I kind of liked that.

Somehow my invented self was becoming a part of my real self, as if I'd somehow caused a dream to breathe.

One day while learning the technical ropes I got a message from something named Humdog.

"What is a Pighed?" it asked me.

I squinted at my screen and typed "!finger humdog," which was the 1993 equivalent of an avatar profile. It was the stats, the hard data, and anything else that individual wanted others to see.

```
Login: humdog                              Name: Carmen Hermosillo
Directory: /home/h/u/humdog                Shell: /usr/local/shell
Last login Fri Sep  8 15:40 1993 (PDT) on pts/56 from adsl-69-225-230-2
Registered: Tue Oct 15 1992
About Me:

    you know everything you want to know already.
```

It was a rather oblique profile she had written. Although Carmen is sometimes a woman's name, I had no clue what I was up against, and since the person had been on the system for almost a year I played it fun. Continuing with my WELL-as-forest idea, I quickly poked back my answer.

"pighed is a bush-shuffler and a root-digger."

I stopped, not sure how much to type.

I continued, "he is new to the forest and is searching for truffles."

This person had been logged in for three hours. What was s/he doing?

Then, hoping to engage a response, I poked, "what is a humdog?"

After a few seconds of staring at a dark screen, new text appeared in front of me, reading, "a humdog sings songs of joy and despair and always has a good nose for finding truffles."

Fourteen years later I would find out how true this was when Carmen was stalked by real-world slave traders via her avatar in Second Life. People near her were kidnapped, died, married; someone was robbed, and other people went off the deep end, disappearing from the system altogether, presumably bound for the nut house. But, as we will see, that would be in 2007, more than a decade later, when our avatars were not simple strings of text but three-dimensional characters who could move, change clothes, exchange gifts, and dance.

WHAT IT IS, PART ONE:
Mario, The Sims and World of Warcraft

The avatar landscape is rocky and full of strange flowers. Here's a page now. I am looking at a small image of a man punching himself in the head. Next to him is Che Guevera. The other images are of lightning striking; a woman with large breasts; a 1950s cartoon of a dancing pig; bouncing breasts (no woman is attached to them this time); a sombrero; Adolph Hitler eating a watermelon; a Pokemon rabbit playing *Dance Dance Revolution*; someone's butt.

These are all avatars.

But what are they?

An avatar is an interactive, social representation of a user.

Avatars are interactive, come in different dimensions, and—like people—they view the world from different perspectives. Sometimes an avatar is a photo, sometimes it's a drawing; it can be based on a real person's appearance or look nothing like them. Usually avatars are a mix of the real and the imagined. They represent an Internet user.

Avatars allow people to interact with a computer system (such as a video game), and/or with other people (such as in online chat environments).

Socially, an avatar represents the user. This is a bit redundant to say, because you don't need representation if there's no one else around, but the social component is important. Examples of social representation are found in chat boards, virtual worlds, and other instances where there's a need for a person to be represented on the screen so that we can keep track of who's who. Without a social environment—or one that at least mimics social interaction—the avatar can't exist. Sociability is the air an avatar needs to breathe.

Avatars are what allow users to interact in social spaces. Maybe it's worth noting that although being social is necessarily interactive, the opposite is not always true: Interactivity is not necessarily social. I can interact with a machine and that might have nothing to do with human interaction. But as far as an avatar is concerned, sociability and interactivity are connected. If it's not social, then why would you need a representation? In the video game Tetris there is no "social" anything. And there's no avatar. But not all systems are like this. Chess is social; is there an avatar? Perhaps. We'll come back to this.

First let's look at avatars and interactivity with the system. There are different kinds of avatars in games just as there are different kinds of characters in movies. A character you see on a computer screen is almost always an avatar.

An avatar is a literary device. It's a protagonist that is used for interactive narratives. Roughly half of all online games use interactive protagonists—characters that allow you to navigate the system. In some games, like Solitaire or Soduku, and in many games that are called "casual games," there is no character, no avatar. These are games that are not narratives as much as they are puzzles. In games, avatars are used to control the story. How the avatar allows the driver to interact with the story is what determines the kind of avatar we're dealing with. Let's survey some examples.

13

Your avatar is a character in a game.

Super Mario Bros. is the bestselling console game of all time. Shipping more than 290 million units, with appearances in more than 100 games, the energetic and polite Mario is something of a cross between an Ewok and James Bond. Pudgy, perky, and sporting a handlebar moustachio, he's a famous hero in the Mushroom Kingdom, where he makes his home. He's got a brother (also a plumber, and also evidently Italian) named Luigi. The brothers are commonly tasked with rescuing a princess. Her name is Peach. She's frequently kidnapped by the evil King, Bowser, and held in a nearby kingdom.

Our plot here is familiar: Rescue the princess.

The avatar is controlled very closely by the player. The player tells Mario when to jump, and where, but the player can't decide how Mario looks, moves, dresses, or emotionally reacts. The control of the story of the game is entirely based on what Mario does. The plot is based entirely on his actions. This simple kind of avatar offers the least control over the story. You're on a railroad track, and you control the speed.

Next let's consider the bestselling PC game of all time. The Sims is a simulation more than a game. The characters in The Sims are more complicated than Mario because most of the game is about creating and managing relationships and doing so within Maslow's Hierarchy of Needs.

The primary characters of the story are the characters the player makes at the beginning of the game: residents of a small house, in a small town, accompanied by a few neighbors. Most often it's a daddy-mommy-baby combination, and the family takes jobs, gets robbed, has parties, goes to the bathroom, and rummages the fridge in the middle of the night—if, that is, the player has provided for such activities. Sometimes neighbors drop by for a visit, and sometimes inconsequential events happen to the Sims while they're at work. In the end, however, the game is about their interaction. It's a social story that's very

popular, and Maxis, the producers of the game, paid for research to find out why it sold more than 25 million units. The results broke users into eight categories. They found that half of the players were female (a first in a video game) and they found out that despite the even division of gender, people fell evenly into four categories.

- The Conformers: First were the people that played the game as it was intended to be played, following the rules and working to generate healthy, happy Sims.
- The Death Dealers: Second group were the people that did just the opposite and killed everyone off or set fires or tried to kill their Sims.
- The Reality Television Viewers: Third were the people who were interested in the strife and drama among the characters—watching the game more than interacting.
- The Doll Housers: Fourth were the materialists who collected furnishings.

Despite being from eight different groups (two genders for each category), three quarters of the users—regardless of gender, or play style— were interested in the interaction between the avatars.

Our basic plot is again familiar: Build a family.

The characters are not controlled by the player, but a player can determine the emotional recipes of each character as he or she is being built. The system guides the social interactions among the characters, and, as with an ant farm, your job is to change their world and see how they react. The control of the story is based largely on decisions players make long before they can see the consequences. For example, I might give a character a hot temper, never thinking he would actually go all the way and kill someone or die as a result of trying. This is an avatar that is a representation of a user, but just barely, and one that is only a little more complex than Mario simply because the user has a steeper learning curve to climb in order to control the story of the game.

14

Then we have the bestselling online game, World of Warcraft. In this bloodbath of a sword-and-sorcery world inhabited by nearly ten million people, a player can choose his or her character's species, job, and gender and can choose from a salad bar of traits that include everything from pointy ears to pointy knives. The player picks the character's armor, weapons, method of movement, skills, and spells that not only personalize the character but allow it to serve as a member of either a competition or a collaboration. For example, whereas a Warrior class needs a Mage class for long-range spell casting, the Mage class needs the Warrior class for hand-to-hand melee. And they both need Priests to heal them when they get hurt. As a result, collaborations form, guilds are built, and the next step is to go and invade the neighbor's turf: Characters work together to form guilds, which then go on raids. Unlike in The Sims, WoW players do not organize parties and then invite the neighbors; they organize parties to get rid of them. Their neighbors are set up in competitive roles so that thousands of people inhabit the same space, see the same events at the same time, and are able to change the state of events and objects in that virtual game world.

Our basic plot is, again, familiar: Beat back the marauding horde.

In World of Warcraft, the user can control how the characters look, how they behave, what they do, and what they say and when, all on the most specific level. The control of the story is very precise, very exact, and it begins to feel much like a movie because there are camera cuts and large panoramas and other characters coming and going. But most all it feels more immersive because it is, because you have things to do—you're in it. The protagonist (that's you) has to speak, move, grab, fight, kiss, and dance.

These games are each interactive narratives. The familiar plots (rescue the princess, raise the family, invade the neighboring kingdom) guide the actions of the player, suggest how to interact with the system, and ask the player to narratively integrate the character within the system of the game. The storyline is clear enough for the player to understand it and interact with it. Consequently, a player will probably not send the Warrior from World of Warcraft to work at the office, just as one would not send the Sims dad into a Berserker stance. It's just not how the story goes. It's not what the character does.

Your avatar allows you to become an interactive character in which you can affect, choose, or change the plot of the story.

Mario, The Sims, and the characters in World of Warcraft are all avatars. These three examples help us see how interactivity and narration work with control and customization and balance one another on a scale that allows the interactive narrative of the game. The control we have over what the avatar does, the degree of customization available in creating and modifying the avatar, and what we do with that avatar all affect the story and how we play with it. You control Mario, but you can't customize him. You customize the Sims, but you can't directly control them. In World of Warcraft you can both control and customize the character.*

We use avatars to interactively represent ourselves, usually in some kind of social environment, generally in a narrative.

Please note the difference in number of users and complexity of avatar: 290 million for the simplest kind of control-only avatar; 25 million for the next simplest (the customized, yet not controlled); and only 10 million for the most complex of avatars that requires the highest technical skill (in World of Warcraft).

WHAT IT IS, PART TWO:
The Three White Girls from YouTube

An avatar is a social creature, dancing on the border between fiction and fact.

Social interaction between online users is what creates avatars, shapes their personalities, and gives them a reason to exist. They don't need to be little 3-D puppets, either.

In 2006 and 2007, on YouTube, LittleLoca, an independent filmmaker and young, attractive woman, began to post videos thanking her fans, doing little dances, and talking about her interests, her family, and the occasional crime of which she'd been a victim with a candor that seemed directed at conveying confidence, pride, and street-savvy sensitivity. Her main message was that she was "keeping it real."

Meanwhile, in Los Angeles, LisaNova, another independent filmmaker, was also busy documenting herself as a young, attractive woman, and she too began to post videos of herself of about ten minutes each. LisaNova appeared to have something of an act to grind, usually against Hollywood stars, and had been gathering a fan base, whom she fed a steady diet of sarcastic impersonations and wry media commentary. LisaNova was interested in impersonations, not in "keeping it real."

Gossip and bickering in any community mean that people are paying attention to one another, but eventually things went sour between these two. LisaNova was Caucasian, blonde, wealthy, and lived on the West Coast. LittleLoca was Latina, brunette, poor, and lived, possibly, in New York. In a welterweight match made for Las Vegas, LisaNova threw the first punch on June 15, 2006, when she posted a fictional impersonation of LittleLoca that parodied LittleLoca's style, dress, behavior, and speech. She even used some of the same filming techniques.

Though *LisaNova's* impersonation was clear, her intent wasn't, and fans of the two women jumped

16

into the fray. Laughter, insults, and flame wars abounded. LittleLoca's only response was "DONT BE FOOLED!! THERE IS A FAKE ACTING LIKE ME!" The situation was complicated by a LisaNova impersonator named LlsaNova, who posted in LittleLoca's forums, and by a LittleLoca impersonator named LlittleLoca, who posted in LisaNova's forums. Things quickly went from catfight to barroom brawl.

Meanwhile, in another part of the YouTube community, a third woman was posting videos of herself as well. Another young, attractive, independent, American filmmaker, she also began to post videos of about ten well-edited minutes each. Bree, or Lonelygirl15, posted videos of herself in her bedroom discussing her thoughts on marriage, boys, parents, and school. She had a secret she was slowly revealing and evidently it had something to do with her parents being part of a religion or cult of some sort.

Her secret was deeper than most people suspected. Eventually, after a great deal of popularity, Richard Rushfield of the *Los Angeles Times* followed up on some rumors fans had been mumbling about. It was discovered that Lonelygirl15 was not American after at all—nor was she a student, nor was she named Bree. She was an actress from New Zealand named Jessica Rose performing a fictional role as a paid professional. The episodic works of fiction she starred in were the brainchild of several fellows from Creative Artists Agency (CAA), a firm run by Los Angeles entertainment executives. They had invented Lonelygirl15 as a media personality, specifically brewed to attract the YouTube audience. After all, LittleLoca and LisaNova had already tested the waters for them, so they knew where to navigate and which rocks to avoid. CAA—very advanced users of the system—set up Lonelygirl15 as an interactive, social representation of a person who didn't exist. She was an avatar in video format.

Viewers, many of them fans of both LittleLoca and LisaNova, were outraged that Lonelygirl15 was actually a concocted scheme rather than a sincere teenager. They weren't angry with the fiction; they were angry with those who created it. Is it ethical to post videos, they asked, that represent someone who doesn't exist? Is it fair to show fiction as fact—or next to fact? And what does this mean for the community? Around this time LisaNova did another impersonation. This time her target was Lonelygirl15 and CAA. The YouTube mob continued to chant slogans, egging on a frenzy involving someone who didn't exist, someone doing impersonations, and someone who was still "keeping it real."

But in reality all three were avatars, and all three were fictional.

LittleLoca wasn't Latina at all but a character played by Stevie Ryan, a white actress from Victorville, California. Ms. Ryan had other avatars, too, named Ooolalaa and TheRealParis, both of which are linked to her "default" avatar, stevieryan.

LisaNova was the avatar of Lisa Donovan, an L.A. actress and filmmaker. Ms. Donovan built an avatar named LisaNova and used her to drive other avatars—Ms. Donovan created fictional renditions of real actors doing renditions of fictional people.

Lonelygirl15 was the avatar of "Bree," but Bree herself was created by professionals as a fictional character. Because CAA were users of the system, Lonelygirl15 was, technically, CAA's avatar's avatar. Lonelygirl15 was an interactive representation of a user specifically designed for the social world of YouTube. This is why users were not angry with the avatar of Lonelygirl15, nor at "Bree, but at CAA.

And as for LlittleLoca and LlsaNova, the random impersonators? They may have been driven by the same person.

The story of the three white girls from YouTube is a collaborative fable played out in a contemporary theater, a social interaction that experimented with fiction and fact as the buttress of the narrative.

An avatar is a narrative device for collaborative fictions.

The three avatars of YouTube shared a social fable. They interacted within the YouTube community, each taking her time onstage and making specific offerings to an admiring public. It was a three-ring circus presenting three different versions of reality from three different perspectives. Fundamentally, it was about the social interaction. Fiction was used to spark debate, create attention, generate interest, and, paradoxically, to "keep it real."

As with reality television, we are finding new narrative formulas of episodic content combining multiple perspectives in a story involving many people. Just as movie actors, celebrities, or rock stars can be both fictional and factual, so can avatars.

Molotov Alva meets his maker, Second Life

WHAT IT IS, PART THREE:
A Point of View

Let's consider the perspectives of different avatars and let's start with the word *profile*.

A profile—that is, the classic, portrait-style profile—is a side view of a person. Profiles are silhouettes, or two-dimensional representations. Social media profiles (on Flickr, YouTube, and so on) or social networking profiles (Facebook, LinkedIn, and the like) are a bit like this as well. They show a relatively flat view of a person or character (real or fictional). The core layout and functionality of the profile is a bit like a baseball card: These avatars have a name, a picture, a few stats, some details about likes and dislikes and usually belong to a "team"—a group of some sort. In systems such as LinkedIn and MySpace, these profiles are collected as friendship links and occasionally sold (recruiters and headhunters, among others, use these systems). Just like baseball cards ome are more valuable than others.

Avatars take different dimensions and give different perspectives.

The sprite-based world of Gaia Online

Now let's consider avatars from a classic shoot-em-up video game, such as Halo or Bioshock. These are first-person shooters. Game-based avatars of this sort are never "seen" as such; instead, the player sees the world of the game from the avatar's perspective. The "camera" for these avatars is mounted on the face. This camera perspective is important and is changing with narrative forms. In movies from the 1950s, the first-person perspective was used to indicate the point of view of a predator (think of Alfred Hitchcock's famous shower scene in *Psycho*). Since most first person shooters are just that it might still represent the predator but it has also started to represent a particular kind of avatar, one that usually has a "dashboard" or "heads-up display" (HUD) indicating that it is an evolved form of the avatar of social networking sites.

We also have a third level of avatar—the second-person camera avatar. These include avatars from either Mario or World of Warcraft. The "camera" floats above the avatar's shoulder, or behind the head. Like puppets or dolls, they live in architectural space. Like the first-person avatar of the console game, they can run, jump, walk, roll, and carry things around, but they are different in that you can, as you drive the avatar, see them do it. These second-person avatars also include the functionality of the first-person avatars as well as the functionality of the profile, or dashboard, avatars.

These dimensionally different avatars have dimensionally different points of view, too, each giving a different perspective on the narrative in which they're involved. This is an important distinction and allows for a kind of taxonomy for avatars.

One of the strangest things about avatars, however—and this may be because they have such vast degrees of control, customization, and can wobble so easily between fiction and fact—is that

there is a *recursive* point of view that allows groups of users to be a single avatar, or groups of avatars to be a single avatar. It is almost as if there are nested avatars inside of avatars, Russian matryoshka dolls that collapse the point of view down to the profile, or baseball card, level. We are now moving into a period of literature when narrative is taking on a fourth-, fifth-, and sixth-person point of view. "God-perspective" games, such as Peter Molyneaux's Black & White or Will Wright's Spore, create multivalent perspectives that allow us the ability to zoom further and further back, giving us new levels of perspective and narrative.

In these bushes is where we can find the answer to the question "Is there an avatar in chess?" The answer is "Yes, and there are more avatars than players." Chess has avatars that exist in both the individual piece (the rook, knight, etc.) and the perspective of the player, both from a high-level, third-person camera point of view, and from the first-person perspective of chess. With this perspective in mind we can better understand the strange Borg-type of avatar named Lonelygirl15. Twitter and group-management systems allow for clustering of avatars, and for the perspectives that float in between. But from here I leave this topic for the hardcore academics and storybuilders to pursue. We don't have the scope to cover such a thing. But Manuel Castells does. His book is titled *The Power of Identity*.

3RD PERSON

2ND PERSON

IST PERSON

20

Lili Brink, Second Life

21

Mortain Bishop, Second Life

22

WHAT IT IS, PART FOUR:
A Simple Character

Regardless of the kind of avatar, the driver of the avatar is involved in a classic tale of character development. The avatar is their character, the system is their story environment, and the events that happen to the avatar are all steps along a narrative chosen by the driver of the avatar. Even in 2-D systems, it is the story and the development of the character—you, in some ways—that keep you returning to the system. The avatar is the protagonist, the protagonist's development comes form events that happen within the system, and the driver of the avatar is the director, actor, and audience.

At its core an avatar is a simple thing. It has a name, a picture, and a social environment. It is an interactive, social representation of a user. Mario or LisaNova, The Sims or Lonelygirl15, LittleLoca or the Master Sergeant, the points of view and the dimensions shift, but the story, for the driver of these avatars, is not unfamiliar. It's the classic arc of character development in literature, in which the character is born, develops, grows, makes friends and enemies, engages in conflict, defines self, and eventually reaches an apex in which one or a few key decisions guide large events. Ultimately, avatars are about the advancement of personality within a kind of fiction that is both social and personal. If I make an avatar, it engages with those of other users and creates a kind of fact about documenting my life—or it makes a kind of fiction that I can share with others. And because avatars are social, other people can do the same to my avatar.

This is the case whenever there is a social, interactive representation of a user. We can see examples in many different avatar-based systems. Social media and social networking sites are just multiuser environments—massively multiplayer online RPGs (role-playing games)—with a different avatar interface. Like video games, social media sites determine what avatars do and present a symbolic or metaphoric method to communicate this. The suggested interaction is embedded in the content. In video games it's the metaphor chosen by the designers that suggests what the avatar does. For example, the guild is preparing to make a raid, suggesting the other avatars respond. In the social media system it's the content chosen by the other users that suggests what the avatar does. LisaNova is busy dishing LittleLoca and Lonelygirl15, suggesting other avatars respond. Ultimately they are all systems where avatars interact over various questions and problems that build the narrative. Most of the Internet is structured to allow avatars of many different sorts to find other avatars, build things, and improve their social standing as a result of doing so. Most of the Internet is a collection of avatar villages.

For myself, I have preferred the immersive, 3-D virtual worlds where I can build things. Making artifacts and stories have been two of my favorite activities through most of my life, and so I gravitate to things like Entropia Universe ("Your Virtual Getaway") or Second Life ("Your World, Your Imagination"). Most of what follows in this book is about this kind of avatar, which, I believe, will become increasingly popular and important as time goes by.

"Why Don't You Spend Time Talking to People in Person?"

"We feel that the defining characteristic of cyberspace is the sharedness of the virtual environment, and not the display technology used to transport users into that environment."
—Chip Morningstar and F. Randall Farmer,
The Lessons of Lucasfilm's Habitat, 1990

In 2002, a company named Linden Lab, based in San Francisco, implemented an idea that had been floating around the Bay Area for almost a decade. It believed that if it offered people the appropriate tools and infrastructure and gave them free access to these tools, users of this system would create a parallel, virtual online world. In a very literal sense, this would be a cyberspace, inhabited by avatars. Linden Lab was banking that users would create new systems of government, transportation, housing, economics, and community. Users would generate the high-heeled shoes, bow ties, top hats, and ivory-tipped canes for high-society avatar gatherings. Users would build the marble hallways, the gold divans, the crystal chandeliers, and the oaken tables. The company believed that users would log in to this system to invent, attend, and manage such gatherings in the first place. Unlike America Online, Linden Lab thought that little structure would be needed, that if they gave people avatars—interactive, social representations of themselves—they would build the world on their own.

They were right.

Nowadays, Linden Lab's creation Second Life is one of many such systems known as an MMORPG (or MMO)—a massively multiplayer online role-playing game. It's a video game with lots of people playing at the same time. Other MMOs include Eve Online, Entropia Universe, AlphaWorld, EverQuest, Lineage, Final Fantasy, Tibia, Pardus, Dofus, Runescape, Asheron's Call, D&D Online, Cybertown, Toontown, WorldsAway, and dozens of others.

These systems are all children of science fiction. In 1992, Neal Stephenson's novel *Snowcrash* appeared, in which users of a computer-based system were able to walk down crowded city streets and talk to virtual versions of one another. This science-fiction dream began to be built out only a few years after the book was published, and after a decade of gestation 3-D seemed to have gone popular. The 3-D dream of *Snowcrash* may not have been quite achieved, but Second Life, or something about it, worked well enough to capture the imaginations of enough people to register more than ten million avatars as of this writing. These avatars have built out more than 270 square miles of virtual land—more than ten times the size of Manhattan.

Before I go on, I'd like to say that the focus on Second Life in this book has to do with my belief that the Second Life system is an important part of what we will see in the coming decade. Fantasy games such as World of Warcraft and Entropia Universe will continue to grow, evolve, and generate more value because, like movies, they carry strong metaphors, give people clear roles, and—more like movies than documentaries—offer strong suspension of disbelief. Although important in this space (it currently holds almost a fifth of the MMO market share), Second Life offers something the others do not: the ability for users to create their own narratives from the ground up. By virtue of being metaphor-free (that is, by not being about spaceships or orcs), it allows us to see a rawer psychology regarding what drives avatars. Other systems such as Multiverse (based on the concept outlined in Stephenson's book), the Ogoglio Project, Areae, and others are also being developed along these lines. I believe we can expect to see more, and most of it from Asia.

Persistent 3-D spaces—online virtual worlds that exist and change regardless of whether you and I are there or not—have been toddling about for a while, in fact, in many facets of pop culture over the past 20 years. For example, in 1985 Dire Straits released "Money for Nothing" as an MTV video using 3-D characters. Ten years later *Toy Story* was released as the first entirely 3-D Hollywood feature, and then, a decade after that, in 2005, Second Life became the fastest growing economy in history, at least for a while.

Dezire and Rraven Moonlight, Second Life

25

Popular culture usually has to do with our ability to get close to it and to "touch" it, and 3-D and virtual worlds give us a chance to do just that. As Erkki Huhtamo, an astute observer of contemporary culture, author, and professor at UCLA puts it, interactive media is a tactile media, and it is because of this— because we can get close to it and touch it—virtual worlds and online games are becoming increasingly popular. Second Life is just one example of this pop-culture appearance of 3-D. It was a cultural commodity we could enter and touch. Second Life offered interfaces to data, to people, and to social networks—to collections of people—with 3-D technologies.

It all orbited the idea of the avatar.

Second Life (www.secondlife.com) may look like a game, but that doesn't mean it is. It's a virtual world, but a world nonetheless. Second Life is more like a continent or city than a game. It is a landscape, one that is populated by avatar cultures as distinct as human cultures.

26

I told my mother about it over the phone one day.

"It's a video game?"

"Well it's like a video game, but we build things and talk to each other in it."

"You talk to each other? In a video game?"

"Yeah," I replied. "It's a 3-D dollhouse world, and we have little puppets we drive to entertain each other. They're called 'avatars.' And there are roles that people play, like actors, a bit like street theater. And we can sell things to each other. Several people made over a hundred thousand dollars this year selling virtual real estate. It's a larger economic system with a larger population than many African nations. And—"

"This is a cyberspace?"

"Yeah."

"Well, I don't understand this stuff you do. Why don't you spend time talking to people in person?"

"I do, Mom. But I also talk with people in other systems. For example, you and I, here on the phone. Why don't we talk in person right now? Because we're too far away, but we still want to talk."

"Okay. I can see that. Well, when you come to visit, I'd like to see it."

"Alright," I said. I like this about my mom; she's always willing to explore. Then there was a pause on her end.

"You're still coming to visit next week, right?"

Sure, we could talk on the phone, but of course, finally, the real world is more important.

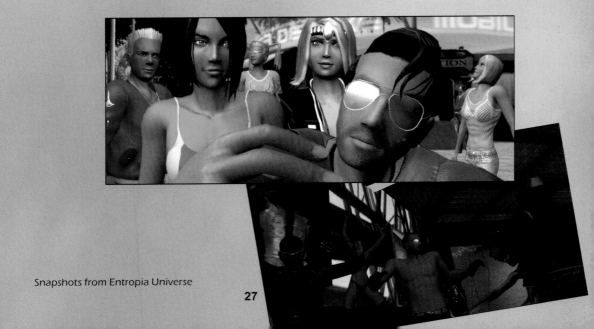

Diving into the Deep End

"Each world while it is attended to is real in its own fashion."
—William James, The Principles Of Psychology, 1890

Merlot Masala, Second Life

When a user logs on to Second Life, they're presented with a bouquet of default avatars to choose from and then customize. In the early days of the system, the default avatar was a rather plastic-looking male or female character. It was bland, Caucasian, and brunette. It was simply dressed in jeans and what might be taken as a cotton T-shirt. This expressionless vanilla avatar quickly reminded one of Ken or Barbie. But it allowed people to enter the system quickly and it gave the user something to work against, creatively. If the new user didn't like being a Ken he could quickly change the length of the nose, slap on a mustache, stretch out the height of the forehead, or make any other of a variety of changes to get the face and body he wanted. Or, conversely, if a new user didn't feel like taking the time or attention that rebuilding might require they could sally forth with this new version of themselves and get right to it.

"It," for me, proved to be very odd.

I remember logging into Second Life initially as a tourist or explorer. Carmen and I had become close friends over the previous ten years, staying in touch via email or other systems we'd visited, and it was she who invited me to this odd place. Carmen has the best nose of anyone I've ever met for online worlds—be it The WELL or Second Life—and she had invited me, and so I went to see.

The initial entry is like most virtual worlds. I plugged in my personal data, including a credit card number, quickly skimmed over a thing called an End User's License Agreement, and unthinkingly clicked Agree. I didn't think the End User's License Agreement (EULA) would be important enough to read, or that the Terms of Service would have any impact on my life, and so, like an immigrant entering a new country with only a vague grasp of the laws, I quickly scrawled my signature on this constitution and boldly stepped into a world whose rules I'd never read.

Initially, like the vast majority of the people who enter these systems, my image of myself was most important to me. My dumb little default avatar—the Ken-looking brunette fellow—had nothing at all to do with me, or who I thought of myself as being. Because I'm a portrait artist, I made my avatar as I make the figures in my paintings: I stretched the body tall, gave him big hands and skinny arms, and evaporated anything that wasn't necessary so that he ended up bony, pale, and graceful. I'd made a smug Davey Jones, a skeletal and snickering ghoul who'd just sauntered fresh off the smoking fields of Tartarus. He was my own tin god, my personal little exemplar. Bony and thin, I imagined him as someone who kept on going even though his body couldn't. Like the figure in many of my paintings, he was spiritual because his body, like a Christian saint, just didn't matter to him. My dumb little avatar had become, on a subconscious level, someone who was spiritual. So spiritual that he didn't even need a body. You could take his body away, down to the bones, and he'd keep on going. I mean, of course he didn't have a body, not really, he was an avatar on a computer screen, but paintings are like that. And I named him Pighed, more out of habit than anything. At this point the name was just natural.

Though I liked the way he looked he was still dressed in the default pants and shirt, and this just wouldn't do, so I deleted his shirt and uploaded a texture that I could use for his pants. I didn't know what to do about his shirt. It looked too pasted on to be believable. All dressed up, but not knowing where to go, I saved my avatar's profile and skipped quickly off to see the world ahead.

The screen went dark. A hissing "you-are-teleporting" sound came out of my computer, and on the screen appeared a strange island where variations on Kens and Barbies were bumping into each other—obviously, other people, like me, who were using the system for the first time and trying to walk. I poked the up arrow on my keyboard and my avatar stepped forward. This was an interface we'd inherited from back in the 1980s, from games like Castle Wolfenstein and Meteor. Everyone knows this stuff. Turn left, turn right, and back up. Page up made my avatar leap into the air, page down brought him back to earth, or ground level, or whatever it was. I poked and prodded until I understood the basics of locomotion.

One of the things I liked about my avatar was that he was a little bit autonomous. He could do the usual things, of course, like put one foot in front of the other while I pushed the up arrow button. He would occasionally look around, or breathe, or blink. He could surprise me a bit. The Second Life system interjects small animations that caused him to scratch himself or strike a pose that might have had emotional implications; a hand on a hip, folded arms, a tapping foot. This slightly autonomous behavior gave me the impression I was dealing with more than just pixels on the screen. I had the impression my avatar was something that was complex, perhaps emotional.

After a little bit I also noticed that I could control these animations. I noticed that embedded in the interface of the Second Life application there were other animations I could use, small gestures I could use to make him do what I wanted. If I dragged an animation icon onto him he would faithfully jump to and carry out the task. He would dance or clap or wave or sit down or eat or sleep or do any other activity I chose. He would bow with English grace or wag his finger with French disdain. So I spent a little time working on animations, making him really express the ideas that came to mind. It was a kind of freedom, though limited, as I still had a lot to learn about the tools. This was a language, I realized, and I was learning the words and phrases. I was learning symbolic, visual words of a language that avatars spoke to one another. The avatars in this system would bow or wag their fingers, and these symbols, just as humans have developed them, meant things that were attached to social cues, pragmatically driven interactions, and the emotions of the person on the other side. Leaning forward with a hand on the stomach indicated respect. Shaking a finger in the air was linked to disdain. Closing only one eye had to do with flirtation. The symbols were all there, though they were a little different, subtler because they were smaller and, for that reason more dramatic as well, like stage acting requires.

Overall the main items in this interface were composed of three primary functions: Talking, moving, and exchanging items. There were dozens of different ways to do dozens of different things, making for a rather complicated screen, but the basics were there and the message was clear: This was a social system built for talking, moving, and trading goods.

With some work, I got my avatar to perform a range of actions from sauntering to leaning to raising one eyebrow to winking. It was while I was working on my shoes, just a few hours after I'd logged into Second Life, that a message appeared on my screen. It was from Carmen, the same Carmen I had met on The WELL in 1993 and who had invited me to try Second Life.

<<Piggie, I am in a little bit of trouble and I need your help.>>
It didn't surprise me. Carmen always got herself into trouble.
<<Oh? What is it?>> I sent back.
<<Well, it's rather complicated. It is called "Gor.">>
The screen was blank for a second as she typed.
An avatar that looked like a blue overfed Carebear walked past me.
<<Basically, Gor>> she continued, <<is a kind of role-play that we do here and I am a slave to a man named Tarl.>>

<<You're a slave? Seriously?>>

<<No, not seriously, it's role play, so it's like a game. Gor is based on a science fiction book by John Norman. In this story there is an alternate world on the other side of the sun where there was a war between men and women, but the women lost, and so they have to be slaves to the men, for all eternity.>>

I raised an eyebrow and scratched my head. I'm not into gender dominance, by either gender, but when you can pick your gender, and when you can decide whether to play or not, then what difference does it make? And anyway, what does it mean to be a slave when you can just turn your computer off? I decided to go along. After all, this was interesting stuff; I had discovered a science-fiction world of Gor that was embedded within a science-fiction world like *Snowcrash*, both of which were embedded in the semi-factual world of Second Life. And Carmen was inventing new forms of fiction within those embedded worlds. It was a hall of fictional mirrors.

Carmen explained to me that I needed to apologize for her, and after a few more quickly coached explanations, a blue panel appeared on the screen, inviting me to teleport to join her. So I clicked it, my screen went dark, and I again heard the "you-are-teleporting" hiss.

The screen lit up, and I saw what appeared to be a glade. Pixilated pine trees swayed slowly in a synthetic wind, mangy astroturf sprouted from the corners of the screen, a rhythmically repeating gurgle played, and I also heard a man's laugh, and then the snap of a whip, and I turned to the right and there was my friend, Carmen—or, rather, her avatar—on her knees in front of another avatar dressed up like Conan the Barbarian. He had it all: the long hair, the broad hairy chest, the chocolaty nipples, the gauntlets, the loincloth. The guy was a steaming hunk of hot avatar action.

Carmen's avatar, meanwhile, was no chopped liver. She was dressed in a gauzy green negligee, a sort of see-through teddy with some jewelry at the appropriate spots. But what was odd about this was that she was on her knees and was wearing a black dog collar.

Whatever they were up to, it appeared to be a kind of personal and very private ritual. I was confused. Though I'd been invited to attend, or perhaps even participate, I wasn't clear on what I was supposed to do. But it was clear that something had to be done. The ritual was surprising for me because my bound friend, in Second Life named Montserrat, is, in the real world, the hotheaded, sassy Cuban habanera named Carmen. This demure milksop slave she was role-playing was not the Carmen I knew. The Conan guy was obviously her master, and above his head floated his name, Tarl. He was acting pompous while Montserrat referred to herself in the third-person as *girl* and asked his apology for being hot-headed and habanera. More private messages (which Tarl could not see) appeared on my screen.

<< Piggie, tell him you are angry with me and that what I did was bad. Please ask him to forgive me on your behalf. It is a very traditional male structure.>>

So I reluctantly said a few bad things about her, even though I had no clue what she had done that was so bad, and then asked Tarl to take her back, though I really had no clue what I was saying.

The message from Carmen appeared again.

<<The technical term for slave is "Kajira.">>

I again tapped out on my keyboard, asking Tarl to take Montserrat back as his Kajira. Though I was smiling and snickering, fortunately my avatar, autonomous as he was, kept a straight face.

It was a ritual of some sort,
but what this all amounted to was still not clear for me.

One thing was clear, however, and that was the emotional intensity of the interaction. There was a privacy that they had, and even in this setting I could not completely step into it. This was no normal interaction. First, the two of them had far too much of a shared vocabulary for normal interactions. They were using words and referring to histories that defined a boundary of private space and shared experience. Second, there were far too many extreme requests being made, of an emotional sort, for this to be a friendship or work-based relationship. When someone asks forgiveness from someone else, there's something heavy happening.

Third, there was an odd reciprocity that was at play: For example, Carmen's obeisance fueled Tarl's dominance, and his dominance fueled her obeisance.

They, or their avatars, or something in between, were in love. Really in love. And it suddenly came clear that these two people had found one another—or found avatars of one another—that allowed them to be who they wanted to be, together. For all I (or Carmen) knew, Tarl was a mother of four in Philadelphia, perhaps, or a 14-year-old boy from Singapore. It was impossible to tell. But I sensed that a strong bond had formed between them, and that this form of role play had crossed some border I'd not yet seen.

After Tarl had accepted her (our?) plea for forgiveness, I asked Carmen what the hell was going on. She explained to me that Gor had several hundred thousand members and that they all played these kinds of roles. I didn't understand how this could happen. How could so many people be involved in such a strange culture. Or was it a society?

When people feign master and slave—arguably two of the most committed roles historically that people in the world have had to bear—and do so willingly, in a virtual world, wrapped in two layers of fiction, then there's something strange going on. Were they just spending too much time online? Did this odd game have to do with the fact that people hide behind their avatars, but at the same time expose their inner feelings—or was it the other way around?

*Willing and unwilling, master and slave,
synthetic and natural, fiction and fact.*

Reality blurred at the first login.

The dream left a bad taste in my morning. After a week or so, I left Second Life and didn't go back for many months, almost a year.

I decided I had better things to do.

The Roles of Social Worlds and the Rules of Game Worlds

There are many kinds of virtual worlds. Each of them is an online interactive system in which multiple people, sometimes millions of people, share in the development of an interactive narrative. (For more on interactive narratives, please see my book *Pause & Effect: The Art of Interactive Narrative*.) Some of these worlds are rendered in high-definition graphics with spatialized audio, and some are rendered in a simple text interface. There are two primary virtual-world genres today: Some are oriented around *social interaction* (such as Second Life), and some are oriented around *game interaction* (such as World of Warcraft). One thing that separates a social world from a game world is the balance of rules and roles.

The rules and roles played in virtual worlds are a key to understanding the importance of avatars.

A rule is a function of mechanics.
A role is a function of theater.

Game worlds are objective-driven systems in which a player tries to achieve a goal under prescribed rule sets. Avatar-based games systems such as World of Warcraft or Eve Online have rules to be played. "Rescue the princess, but don't get killed. If you get killed, you start over. Earn points to go up levels. You get more power with each level." These rules offer objectives, challenges, and methods for playing games. The rules are there to be discovered as the game is played. This is what most classic "video games" are about. Generally speaking, if you follow the rules of the game, you achieve the goals of the game.

Rules frame interaction with the machine (the software, system, or game).

Social worlds are socially driven systems in which a player tries to achieve social position under emergent rule sets. Avatar-based social world systems such as Second Life, or There, have roles to be played. "Create drama for fun and education. Make friends that matter. Navigate the line between compliment and criticism." Roles are slightly less distinct, slightly more flexible, and almost entirely social. They offer community, goals, commerce, and a structured method of interacting that allows players in virtual worlds to understand what needs to be done. Some examples of roles might be a bartender, a shopkeeper, a shoe salesman, a bouncer, or a slave. They might be a master, an advisor, a pickpocket, or a joker. They do not earn points, other than the invisible benefits of societal living. How well you integrate into your little society depends on how well you play your role. Roles are there to frame interaction with the community (the society, or the group).

Roles frame interaction with the community.

In some systems, weights might be needed more than wings. In Second Life—where you can fly, create castles with the wave of your hand, and talk to people from infinite distances—extremely hierarchical systems of both rules and roles get quickly introduced. The slave-based world of Gor might be able to flourish in a system like Second Life precisely because there is so much potential freedom.

Maybe the more freedom we have, the more rules and roles we need to invent.

Young Geoffrion, Second Life

The Assumption of The Mask

The avatar is a tool for regulating intimacy.

Human beings have a profound need to connect. We will travel great distances, give expensive presents, wait in long lines, and endure odd hardships of emotional immolation to achieve connection with other people. This desire is part of what makes avatar-driven systems so powerful, because when we are using our avatars online we feel emotionally safer to connect, and also more protected in doing so. Avatars are an amazing way of controlling the intensity of intimacy. This is why some people prefer Second Life and systems like it to the real world. Their intimacy and interaction with others can be more easily controlled, and they feel more protected.

We feel safer because the person we are talking to is not right next to us, because they cannot see our real faces, because we cannot see theirs, and because, perhaps, they have no idea even who we are. We feel safer because at any time, we tell ourselves, we can turn off the computer, get up, and go outside. We're not entirely connected, we tell ourselves. We can unplug at any time.

Over 75 percent of Internet users feel safer speaking their mind when they use an avatar.

But in fact we are more exposed precisely because we feel this way. We are more inclined to reveal ourselves when we use our avatars. We're more inclined to reveal what we want, dislike, and think. We are more inclined to expose ourselves on the assumption that anonymity and distance matter. But in a world where information is more important than physical proximity, we are not as safe as we might assume. As I will get into later, I have seen some extreme tragedies unfold because of the assumption of the mask. This intensity makes the potential for emotional involvement quite real. Because we can immerse ourselves more and more into these environments, we let our guards down.

Most users, when they build their avatar, arrive at an alternate, less protected version of themselves. In Carmen's case, the persona

36

Aponi Yifu
Second Life

she had made was Montserrat; for me it was Pighed. We put these masks on, entered our virtual worlds, and had the feeling is that "all is under control." After all, the word *persona* originally meant, in ancient Greek, "mask." Not as in a thing that hides your face, but one that shows what is truly underneath. Wearing this mask helps us feel as if things are really under control, but it is not necessarily true. There are many indications that we have much less control as we use avatars than we might think. The number of hours alone that people spend in systems such as Second Life is a good indicator that they are more powerful than TV or other media. I, for example, spent days in Second Life and never stopped other than to sleep. I've never done that with television, radio, movies, or the Internet.

When we are revealing what we want, dislike, and think, it is easier for us to be interpreted, modeled, and manipulated. And many people in virtual worlds are there to do just that. I've met, in my travels through Second Life, benevolent inquisitors such as research students and people who were trying to understand what their lover had found in-world. But I've also met corporate marketers and slave masters.

Alts, Newbs, and How a Fisherman Gets Fresh Fish

After some nine months or so, a good while after I'd last been in Second Life, I dipped back in for a look. I'd been lounging about in other virtual world systems, trying airplanes and taking on gunslingers, an Orc here, an Elf there. But Second Life still seemed new to me and had a kind of draw the others didn't because of its flexibility. I'd never seen another virtual world where there was absolutely no narrative metaphor. I'd never seen a princess, Boba Fett, and a poodle-carrying Marine all hanging around together talking about the real U.S. president. I'd never seen such metaphor-free worlds where people just did what they fancied. But that apparently included the thing I'd seen in Gor, the slave ritual that Carmen and her buddy were involved in. That in particular stuck in my memory like a burr, and I knew it was important. Like any trip to a far-flung land, it was strange enough to be fun and strange enough to be dangerous. In fact, it was so strange that I was disgusted by it.

Disgust is reason to investigate. It usually indicates some kind of ignorance. It usually means there is something to learn. Now, I was definitely disgusted by the slave thing, but I would tell myself it was okay. I would tell myself the very thing I told you: "Oh, it's okay, because you can be whatever gender you want to be, so there aren't really slaves." The very concept of slavery made me feel a little grimy. The only solution was for me to go back in and have a look around—as a woman slave. I knew I couldn't go anywhere near as deep as had Carmen swum. But I did take a peek.

I made a secondary avatar, a non-Pighed avatar.

These secondary avatars are generally called *alts*. Once you get used to the system and know what to look for, they're relatively easy to spot. They carry a recent birthday, yet they also carry a large number of accessories that take a long time to collect. Sometimes the alt is a member of a group that requires long-term role play or deep technical knowledge. If you keep a sharp eye out you can see them. Meeting one is a bit like meeting a teenager who drives a 1968 Ferrari and has competed in world-class racing events. You can tell something is amiss.

I built my alt carefully, to avoid these things. I added no accessories, joined no groups, gave no indication that this avatar was anything other than a very recent account by a very new user. It was to appear as a *newb* account.

Picking the default Barbie avatar with the blue jeans, blue eyes, and the tight-fitting purple top, I stood around in the welcome area for a while. Once I got there, I changed my hair to blonde and increased my breast size a bit. I felt like Christina Aguilera. There was one other avatar that looked like me, but with smaller breasts. I felt socially camouflaged.

It was a strange scene, like the *Star Wars* cantina, full of people from all over, no one doing much more than chewing the fat. There was a man with the head of a wolf, a robot that carried a gun, a muscle-bound Zeus of a fellow, complete with toga and accompanied by a Hera. He wasn't what I was looking for. Someone with flashing eyes and ribbons streaming behind them flew over the two teddy-bear twins who were dancing in the courtyard near the fountain. Eventually I found him: a guy dressed up like Conan. If it was a him, that is. It was an excellent-looking avatar. The muscles were well defined, his skin had a sweaty shine to it, the clothes had small stitching woven in—even his hat (a war helmet with horns on the side) had a bit of fuzz around the base. He carried two swords and a quiver of arrows. I went over to stand nearby and intentionally walked into a tree. I stood there for a second, looked at the tree, and rotated in a 90-degree angle.

"Hey there," he typed. It read like a drawl.

"Hi!! How r u?" I poked back. I figured that if I mimicked an overexcited girl, maybe around 19 or 20 years old, he'd take the bait.

"Good, good… You new here? Need a hand with something?"

It was so typical I slapped my forehead in real life. Now, naturally, this was a situation a bit like a bar. I was like a hot young thang who had just wandered in out of the rain with a broken umbrella, and this guy had just offered to buy me a drink. We were reading lines from someone's script, but I had no idea whose.

"How do I teleport? What do we see!? Where r we!?"

I listened, for the next 30 minutes, to a well-crafted monologue of how Second Life is an environment that follows a close story: The men are masters, the women are slaves. It takes place on a world opposite the sun. That, he told me, is what Second Life was about. *All* of Second Life. If I wanted to play the game, I needed to be a slave. And he could show me how. To "learn how to play Second Life," I needed to stick with him. He gave me some new clothes and some animations to use. He gave me some money. He gave me a very pretty bodice. As the teddy bear twins continued to dance in the courtyard, I asked him about the other avatars—who were they? He explained (that is, lied) that these other avatars were simply people experimenting. The "Real SL Players" were the Goreans.

Despite what my profile said, I wasn't born yesterday. This chap was out collecting slaves, and though I wasn't buying it, I was encouraging him to sell. In that way, I was a liar too. It's worth noting that just as I had swapped my gender, for all I knew, this Conan-Man could have been a grandmother in Missouri. Our interaction, our lies, our odd script, and the psychological strings that were being pulled were all connected to the avatars. It was a strange interaction that was cued and guided entirely by our little characters.

By the end of the day I had abandoned my alt account, this time with a new set of disgusts, concluding that hanging out in the newb areas is how some Goreans go about finding new meat. The "prey" enter on their first day, and the "predator" shows up to invite them to learn the deeper workings of the system. These experienced Gorean players offer presents, compliments, secrets, and cues into the social workings of the virtual world. A little tour around the neighborhood, a little pocket change, a smile here and there, and I'd think I'd found a new friend. After all, that seemed to be the way Carmen, my trusted friend of more than a decade, had initially guided me. But this guy had hidden intentions. His ultimate goal was to sculpt a new player into assuming a particular role so that he, in turn, could play out his particular role.

And it works, for obvious reasons. Most women enter Second Life with a female avatar. Most women (and men) start with a desire to be connected to a society and make a friend or two. Having someone we can trust in a new world is a common wish. After all, we all want to feel connected. One of the first things we do when we move into a new neighborhood is talk with the neighbors, exchange gifts, and learn how things are done locally. This very human, social process helps us identify our clans, groups, friends, and families—and, therefore, our identities. This was certainly the case with my early days on AOL. I was a member of the pig crew. We were a clan of sorts, and it was that attachment to community that encouraged me to return day after day, at least in part. The same was true for the Goreans and the poor newbs who got caught up in their role-play systems of slavery, unwary of the potent psychological cues hanging from an avatar.

Adept at psychological manipulation, the Gorean slave master knows that a bewildered person will be first to trust. He's there to help. But to be fair, most of the women in Gor who become slaves volunteered to do so. And anyway, an experienced player, and especially an experienced Fisherman, can tell the gender of the player as something separate from the gender of the avatar. But of course the gender of the person driving the avatar doesn't matter, does it. Or does it?

Carmen says that you can tell a real man from the size of his breasts. Specifically, the size of his nipples.

When they make their female avatars, men tend to make the nipples very large. They do what drag queens do—they get "hyper feminine." Bigger hair, perfect makeup, more expensive skin, flimsier silks, sluttier language. Carmen's told me that, by her estimate, about half of the slaves in Gor are real-life males. This is something that she says is assumed by most of the population. Another assumption is that most of these men are gay. Some masters refuse to have a slave until they've spoken with the slave on the phone. Some masters have a rule that in order to be a slave on his island, you have to be at least 45 days old.

Some people build entire clubs full of alts. There was a group made of only alts, a club with a name like Slavery Madness, where all the avatars in the group were controlled by the same person. I've heard of people who run two avatars simultaneously. And a man named Saajuk told me that he knows a man who is his own Gorean master.

These things are strange enough to be fun and strange enough to be dangerous. Strange enough that, because of the strange nature of avatars, if I ever had to watch someone apologize to himself in a forest glade I'd probably log out in disgust.

Falcon Nacon, Second Life

FUR VS. GOR

There have always, of course, been many avatar societies in Second Life. Just like downtown L.A., a connection point of many highways from far away, a world trafficked by people from all walks of life, driving along highways that split and rejoin, spewing out avatars into central catchbins, blending individual cultures into a bizarre patchwork society. Second Life usually felt, for this reason, urban.

If the Goreans were the hyperborean, heterosexual, far-right conservative Christians and capitalists who followed their own rules to the hilt, then the Furs, or Furries, were the hypermodern, homosexual, far-left liberal Shintoists and commies who loved being wild in the wilderness.

Fur Nation, or Furry Fandom, was a Second Life avatar society of animal characters with human characteristics. Furry Fandom, like the *Snowcrash* fiction, or the fiction of Gor, also originated with literary fiction—some say with books such as Richard Adam's famous novel *Watership Down*, or even going as far back as the Egyptian myths of bipedal animal-gods such as Anubis, Bast, or Horus. There are other claimed sources of Furry origin, such as from 1990s New York City masquerade balls. People would show up at the parties in animal outfits, doused in pheromones, and engage in anonymous sex while more or less wearing their animal outfits. Whatever its origin, just as Second Life had a strong subculture of Goreans, it also had a strong subculture of Furs.

Furry avatars were also very well made, with fine attention to detail. They came in all shapes and sizes, but were almost always bipedal and almost always had the head of a totem animal. Whereas the Goreans generally looked as photorealistically human as the system would allow, the Furs were mostly feral. A goat head, a fox head, a set of wings here, a tail there, piercings and tattoos, hair and horns, armor and bling, tattoos and texture maps, the Furs were out to take full advantage of whatever the system could offer. I have seen dragon colonies where four-story tall avatars meander about talking about real-world politics while blowing virtual smoke through their dragon-noses. I spent an afternoon talking with a group of mouse-headed men, all of whom were sporting erections the size of baseball bats. There was the forest where I met the pig people (and was quite happy to have my own Pighedded avatar). And there was the afternoon spent on the cloud, where the entire village was comprised of rat-headed angel avatars, all immaculate and dressed in white.

40

Sara Kochav, Second Life

But the Goreans and the Furries didn't usually get along. In fact, the two cultures were closely matched opposites. The Goreans were intensely and completely hierarchical; the Furs were not. The Gorean avatars practiced exclusively hetero sex; the Fur avatars were bisexual. The Gorean metaphor was based on ancient Western history; the Furs used a collection of metaphors that were based on emerging modernity. The Goreans tailored their language to a very specific set of rules, such as saying "Tal" when greeting one another; Furs rarely had such rules. Goreans were deeply involved in psychological role play; Furs preferred the technology.

But, oddly, both practiced slavery, and both used the same word for it: Kajira.

The differences between the two tribes seemed to smolder and kindle until eventually a series of small wars broke out on several islands.

The Goreans and The Furs both used their respective weapons, both informational.

The Goreans, masters of deception and manipulation, used psychological tactics. These usually involved dressing up as a Fur, visiting a Furry town, sparking a few well-placed rumors or outright lies, and then using these to drive divisions within the Fur society. The goal was to sow mistrust and create rifts between friends of common fur. It usually worked. After all, in Second Life, it was occasionally difficult to know whom to trust, so sowing mistrust was about as easy as growing weeds.

The Furs, by way of retaliation, used their own arsenal—a technical command of the system, rather than a psychological one. Generally speaking, Furs are more alert to things like server latency and packet loss, and a superior technical knowledge led some of them to the creation of well-known black-market weapons. These were simple devices that were sold via off-world sites such as SL Boutique, or SL Exchange. Listening devices or bugs were planted, but soon the Furs were able to crash servers by creating small items that would clone themselves again and again until the server wasn't able to handle the load. It was a bit like forcing someone out of their home by introducing a strain of quickly reproducing rabbits; the overpopulation soon leaves no room for anything else.

So the Goreans planted rumors, and the Furs planted scripts, and the conflict grew tall.

One day I asked a friend of mine, a Fur, why these skirmishes were taking place.

"We're a little too much alike, I guess. A little definition is needed."

On an island named Eponia, there was a population of Furs that practiced Gorean rituals: Animal-headed folk who had strict social hierarchies and severe domination roles. This drove both the Furs and the Goreans crazy. It was owned and managed by a Gorean slave (when she was not too busy being a pony). Then there were the Gorean girls, from strictly Gorean islands, that sported Fur accessories as a kind of fetish—tails, ears, little tufts of hair on the back end. That drove everyone crazy, too. Eventually a war broke out, and its function was to define ownership of boundaries.

VIRTUAL WARS

1angelcares Writer, Second Life

42

This kind of war was about establishing boundaries of identity and culture. It happens in many different kinds of systems, with many different kinds of avatars. On a sunny Tuesday afternoon, in the real world, I shared some tea with a friend of mine named Silvio. We were discussing his account on Flickr. He had encountered a similar kind of Gor-Fur battle between Flickr avatars.

"When I started, I was cautious not to share my thoughts with anyone there," he said. "Then I thought, I'm not the kind of guy who fucks around and I don't care if [people on Flickr] believe in God or eat meat or are a vegetarian. I found that a lot of people were really opinionated. They would pick fights left and right over stupid crap. And some of these people would push me, probably because I would never fight. But I felt pushed and instead of getting angry I became "Milvio." Then I started really talking about my point of view and I wanted people to know who I was. I wasn't there to play a game any more."

I asked Silvio what he meant by "play a game."

"Before [these fights], I was always there to just be me. But if you put people on an island—even best friends—eventually fights and backstabbing start. This is what I've seen in any community."

An avatar is an identity container, one with boundaries. When those boundaries are challenged, battles break out at the border.

From the personality wars of Flickr to the Gor versus Fur wars of Second Life, avatar wars are wars, which although bloodless, are somewhat like the ones in the real world. One difference is that with avatars, the motive is to define the boundaries of identity rather than the boundaries of land. From the desire to be part of a community, to the groups and tribes that are formed as a result of this desire, tribes and families arise. And from them a need for self-definition appears. And when that self-definition doesn't happen easily, conflict occurs.

As a result of these conflicts, new cultures emerge. They are like little villages, or city-states, made up avatars who have established a specific definition of who they are and are not. These city-states develop history and culture, and when they are devalued, or when their citizens feel their identity isn't being acknowledged, fights happen. For example, on April 29, 1992, in L. A., when the Rodney King riots got rolling, the issue was largely one of racial oppression and the preferential treatment of whites. The four days of riots were about that group of Angelenos insisting on the validity of their identity and their proper treatment in the society. In virtual worlds, fights happen over differences in behavior (which, ultimately, could be the case in real-world examples). After all, the "land" in virtual worlds is there merely to frame the avatars. What's important, and what people find worth fighting over, are the boundaries of those avatar city-states, defined by behavior, communication methods, and rituals.

RITUALS AND ARCHETYPES

People put on masks of ritual and role and build new kinds of culture. A culture, like a city-state, is a group identity that sometimes needs to be defended. But the definition of that culture, like that of any city-state, happens not only outside the walls but inside them as well.

Though the wars were fought at the boundaries of group identity, those avatars within the borders of the culture seemed to get along quite well. They had strong bonds, solid rituals, a diverse range of roles, and a clear sense of why they were there. Within their culture, the members heartily agreed with one another about who they were and how to stay that way. These agreements had to do with behavior, and they appeared in many forms. Some of the agreements were clear and evident, such as how avatars should dress and behave. On all Gorean islands that I know of, for example, it was explicitly forbidden to look anything other than a human from pre-Renaissance Europe. The avatar needed to not only look human, it needed to be dressed in typical sword-and-sorcery leather or lace. Welcome signs told you this, and explained other rules, when you teleported in to any of the Gorean Islands.

The fact that all the "guys" dressed in medieval leather and all the "girls" dressed in saucy see-throughs was easy to pick up on when you entered the space, even without signs. It was strictly forbidden to look like a Furry (or a robot, or a spaceman, or whatever). The agreements of this culture also demanded that the members speak and even move in certain ways. Flying, for example, was not allowed on Gorean islands. The agreements were there for the members of the group to recognize the kind of behavior that

was allowed, and what ideas, words, actions, and interactions were and were not part of their emerging culture. These agreements on what kind of behavior was appropriate bordered on a kind of morality.

The rituals were built out of rules and roles.

Some of these agreements (such as dress code) were evident and simple. Others, however, were subtle and quite complicated. An example is the Gorean wedding. In Second Life, weddings (and divorces, for that matter) are commonplace and happen at a much faster rate than in the real world. People may be married only for a few weeks. A Gorean wedding, or Free Companion Ceremony, was a like a real-world wedding in that there were fancy clothes, and an officiating person, and a church of sorts, and people sat in rows to watch. But a Gorean wedding would only officially last for a real-life year and was also a bit different than a standard wedding. They had their own clothes, of course, and used certain music. It was all a bit medieval: The food was typically turkey legs and whole pigs with apples in their mouths. Not the sort of food that is commonly served at a Western wedding anymore. These Gorean role players refined the words of the wedding to their own culture, and they had special dances that were, I understand, very, very specific. A dance was an animation that someone else made, so the avatar couldn't mess up the move. These things are all rituals that helped to define the culture they had invented.

44

My introduction to both Gor and Fur was via ritual. My introduction to Gor was the ritual of Montserrat-Carmen on her knees, asking for forgiveness from Tarl in the forest. My introduction to Fur was also in a forest, but it was a crazed monkey chase scene that took place up in the branches and was similar to a game of tag. These two rituals were each definitions, to some degree, of these respective cultures. In Gor the hierarchically driven interaction between members (and what level an individual could climb to), determined the underpinnings of the society. Among the Furs, the more free-form kind of play and less structured form of interaction was emblematic of that culture.

This kind of thing is just what people do, whether we drive avatars or not. People perform these kinds of little agreements all the time, regardless of age, location, gender, or social context. Consider the handshake. Here in Los Angeles, I've seen kids on the street shake hands, point their thumbs in the air, and bump fists. In Paris I've seen kids of the same age shake hands, slap their hand to their own chest, and then touch elbows. It is a physical way of interacting to say, "We are part of the same group, and we both know it, and we can prove it in our interactions." Avatars represent their users in exactly the same way. It's a basic and integral interaction that represents the user and their cultural role.

Just as rituals help define culture, avatar rituals help define avatar cultures. The analogy to shaking hands might be a word that is typed (such as "Tal") or an animation that is initiated (such as a hug). But the rituals are more important in virtual worlds than in the real world. In a virtual world we don't have some of the same degree of complexity or fidelity of the senses. Given the technology that virtual worlds use, subtleties in human behavior are lost (or translated to other subtleties). And so avatars have to make up for it in other ways, usually by one of these greeting rituals, though it can happen in other situations, depending on what the group likes and invents. That is how the behavior of avatars helps to create rituals.

Archetypes, too, are created by behavior, as well as appearance. The Hero and the Guide are two common archetypes found in literature and movies, and it's pretty easy to tell them apart because they neither look nor act alike. For example, Luke Skywalker (the Hero) doesn't look like Obi-Wan Kenobi (the Guide), and Luke doesn't act like Obi-Wan, either. Their appearance and behavior define them as different archetypes. They are personalities and identities we can point to and identify as archetypes because of their behavior. Avatar designs, both visually and in terms of how they behave, tend to orbit archetypes of one sort or another. The Hero, the Baby, the Guide, the Child, the Sage, and so on.

Avatars represent an archetype of a very personal sort, and these archetypes are linked to the rituals that avatar groups build. The cultural rituals of Gor, Fur, and the other cultures I came across were dominated by archetypal avatars. In a virtual world, the only things we can exchange are symbols. These symbols, whether they are interactions and rituals or actions and archetypes, become the community's defining text.

Because an archetype has to do with personality and behavior, and because rituals contain behaviors and require specific sorts of personalities, rituals give archetypes meaning and expression, and vice-versa. The visual representation that a person chooses for their avatar has something to do with their role in the society. This is part of what archetype means. That day in the glade, I saw this Conan the Barbarian slave master named Tarl. The visual barbarian archetype mapped well to the behavioral ritual of the slave master. Tarl looked like someone that would dominate and rule in a very physical way. Of course, this avatar was no more "physically" powerful than was Carmen's— neither of them was physical at all, of course—but by appearing that way, by presenting the visual symbols of physical power, it was easier for both of them to accept the ritual. It would be hard to do otherwise. With names like Tarl and Montserrat, I would have a hard time imagining these two doing anything else. The barbarian and the trampled

45

princess were deep in their roles, and I certainly didn't expect either them to begin discussing something out-of-role, such as homosexual anonymity or automotive repair.

Dress, body shape, action, interaction, words, and all other symbols and elements of their roles and rules were strictly pre-determined boundaries, and it is within these boundaries that most avatars live. In Second Life, archetypes are defined by the people driving the avatars. In World of Warcraft the archetypes and rituals are more defined by the designers of the system. In Eve Online, the avatars are spaceships. But regardless of the system, it is within that cultural set of archetypes and rituals that the avatar lives.

Avatar rituals encourage archetypes, and archetypes encourage rituals, and with these instruments in each hand the avatar plays the songs of personality and narrative.

Kirana Rowley
Second Life

The Dive into the Deep End Continues

Carmen and I had both died and been rebooted.

Many moons had passed since my gender-bending fisherman experiment. During the intervening months I spent time in Eve Online, Gaia, EverQuest, and other virtual worlds. But Second Life attracted my inner anarchist. I decided to log back in, see if I could earn some money from the effort of spending time in there (which I knew would be considerable), watch how people were getting by, learn what I could about interactive forms of narrative, and investigate these avatar societies. Those were my motivations as an immigrant.

In the months that followed I became a builder named Pighed Stonecutter. I built houses, furnishings, skins, body shapes, clothes, and terraformed the islands and ground that avatars would use. Metaphorically speaking, my role was to make the avatars' playing fields. I suppose I knew it when I logged in, because that's what I've always done in these systems. Even as a kid, when I'd play Dungeons & Dragons I always preferred the role of the dungeon master—the guy who builds the environments and carves out the narratives for people there. Since Second Life provided the last name, and I had to pick one, "Stonecutter" seemed appropriate.

As for Carmen, it was with huge pleasure I found that Montserrat the Slave had died (or rather committed virtual suicide) and been reborn as Sparrowhawk Perhaps. She was a little more like herself now, too. She was still sexy and curvy, all buxom and classic, the Gothic gardenia of her imagined self, but she had also purchased an island called Shivar, installed herself as a "reluctant queen," and had begun a new life. From slave to queen, she had gone through quite a role reversal. She gave me the title Prince of Tenaya (which helped frame my role), L$1000 (Linden dollars, the Second Life currency) so I could get properly

47

dressed, a little land, and a bouquet of instant friends (all quite interesting people, and no slaves or masters). And then she set me off, saying, "Build your home." I remember looking at my SL bank account as I might if there were doubloons in my palm, and then calculated that she had given me about US$3, which was enough to buy pretty much anything I'd want—at least anything I'd want to get started, that is.

Evidently, I'd been born into nobility.

And there, on the coast of Shivar, is where my story began. I had friends and family. I had a job and a little bit of money. I felt as if I could make something of myself, and that was precisely what I set about doing.

Second Life and many virtual-world societies can be cold places unless you already know people in the system who will help you get going, and it doesn't help if one is simply looking at architecture blander than Los Angeles tract housing. In order to enter any society, one must have a role. You must know something about the rituals and archetypes. You must have something to do there. It is best if you have something to contribute, and it helps if you have a place to call home, where you can spend time with friends you know and trust. Just as in the real world, getting around can be tricky, and it takes a while to find your way. This situation is a huge problem for tourists and researchers. They have little to give, so they get little in return. Most virtual worlds function like this, and most unfavorable reviews neglect this societal factor.

When I saw my avatar again, I realized I had work to do. I got back to work on my little self-portrait of a ghoul, knowing that if I were going to spend some time with this thing, then I really needed to put some energy into the design. It would, after all, become "me." Part of my energy had to do with pride, but part of it also had to do with exhibitionism. As an exhibiting artist I knew how to make a fine avatar, and so I spent a good day working on learning the system well enough to build my skin: a pale blue parchment covered with tattoos of a Chinese astrology chart that marked the day my avatar was born. I threw a Fu Manchu mustache in, tweaked the body further with a skinnier neck, bigger hands, and bonier knees—then, for good measure I drew a big blue circle around the eyes to add to the skull look a bit. In real life I have broad shoulders and a thick neck and most people assume I'm either a thug or a sports fan, so I made my avatar slumped, thin, and unhealthy-looking. I popped a cigarette in his mouth. And I left the shirt off. Better to show my tattoos and skinny chest, I decided.

If I was going to be a builder, I needed to build. I went down to the beach and began to play around with the modeling system, piling a large architectural mess of spirals and twists on top of each other. Eventually, with a little organization, I made several simple room-platforms and a kind of lookout tower and, because I was the Prince of Tenaya, named it Tenaya Spirals. I put out a couple pieces of furniture, sat down, and looked out at the synthetic sea below the tower. An animation moved the water along, giving the impression of swells coming down the coast. I could hear an audio file of wind from time to time. (The islands in Second Life actually had weather modeled into them; sometimes it was windier than others.) The ocean below seemed alien. But that was to be expected. That is always what immigration feels like.

In the weeks that followed I met a few people, flew around a lot, and started to collect odd things (guns, soda cans, a table with a turkey on it, a necklace, a little pink pig). I spent most of my time at Tenaya Spirals, where I passed the days building accessories or furniture or odd

48

things that just couldn't exist in the real world, like inside-out cubes that spun in the middle of the air.

But because my avatar was the most important thing I'd built in the system—which is the case with most people who spend time in virtual worlds—I continued to fine-tune him, too. I built custom animations and whittled his face into a slightly more chiseled version of what I had imagined. Was it his face or my own? The line was getting less distinct as I met more and more people. They knew me only as they saw me, and what they saw was the avatar I built. And as I continued with these small refinements, he continued to change underneath me, a bit like my own body in my own real life. Sometimes I feel like I'm too fat, so I exercise and drop it. Sometimes I cut my hair or shave and then check these small changes in the mirror. The parallels with my avatar were interesting, but I didn't spend much time dwelling on them. It wasn't really my life, and it wasn't really my body. Or so I thought at the time.

Sparrowhawk-Carmen would come over and we would sit down and talk for hours on end about love, or history, or books, or what it means to enjoy a virtual glass of virtual wine and watch a virtual sunset. We would talk about whether or not the brain, stuck inside its dark, dank lockbox of a skull where only electrical signals pass in and out, can differentiate between the real and the virtual. We would talk about Tarl, the one she'd had to bow down to, who was having an impact on her life, and how even though she had a new avatar their relationship had continued. We would talk about how love does not need to be a thing that is in the real world. People have married who once were pen pals; phone relationships have blossomed into weddings; online dating has created all kinds of waves in the emotional landscape of people's lives. We considered that romantic love may be best where there are no real concerns. The body might be a bit overrated, we wondered. And we talked about these things and sat with our virtual legs dangling over the virtual cliff below, or stood together in one of the lookouts of Tenaya Spirals. As we watched the cold, fake sun cast its neon orange glow across the ripples of a synthesized sea, we talked about real things, real emotions, and real people. But we did it there, in-world.

The Various Iterations of Pighed Stonecutter

It was one evening, after she'd left, and after I'd stayed at Tenaya Spirals looking out over the cliffs at the small ripples in the ocean below, that I noticed it was really quite lovely.

And it was also then that I noticed that…

In staring out into space I'd fallen over the deep end.

The line between the virtual and the real was getting thinner by the week.

49

ON DRINKING VIRTUAL WINE
AND THE GROUNDING OF BELIEF

We understand media as reality. We interact, emotionally, with another avatar as we do with another real person. And for some people an avatar is a more convincing reality than a real person

In 1996 Byron Reeves and Clifford Nass, two Stanford University professors, wrote a book called *The Media Equation*. The media equation, simply put, is an equals sign: Media experiences equal real-life experiences. They argued that this is true not just for interactive media, but for all media. After years of research and hundreds of interviews, their core argument was that people assume what they see in media is reality because evolution never demanded our brains do otherwise. Our media has out-evolved our brains, and so fiction registers, on a subconscious level, as fact. Our brains evolved in a world where only humans did human things. Reeves and Nass point out many interesting things that apply to avatars and our experiences in virtual worlds and games. One example is that fictional characters in media can actually invade our personal space. Just as a real person can stand too close and cause a strong emotional response, so too can avatars. Attention, memory, reaction time, and emotions are all affected by whether a virtual character is close or far away from a real living person. This has been known for decades by film and television directors; the closer the camera is to the subject's face, the stronger the emotional relation the viewer has with the subject. But it's true for avatars as well. Jeremy Bailenson, a cognitive psychologist and also a Stanford professor, has noted (as well as other virtual-worlds observers) that people tend to stand more or less the same distance apart in virtual worlds as they do normally in real life. Others have noted that if an avatar tells someone that a thing is true or untrue, good or bad, real or false, a human on the other end of the screen will believe it.

Psychologically, you are your avatar.

"People respond to interactive technology on social and emotional levels much more than we ever thought," says Reeves. "People feel bad when something bad happens to their avatar, and they feel quite good when something good happens." It might be even stronger than that, however. For example, Nick Yee, a recent Ph.D. graduate, also from Stanford, conducted a survey of 30,000 gamers. He found that approximately 40 percent of men and 53 percent of women who spend time in virtual worlds said their virtual friends were equal to or better than their real-life friends. Most of these people spent more than 20 hours a week in virtual worlds, and of these folks a quarter said that the highlight of their past week had happened while they were using their avatar.

But wait, there's more. Research suggests that humans can even be convinced by an avatar to commit real-life murder.

Goblin Oh, Second Life

Back in the 1960s, Stanley Milgrom, at Yale, conducted a series of tests on authority and murder. In 2006, a collection of researchers in Europe imported Milgrom's experiments into virtual worlds. At the Department of Computer Science, University College London, researchers used avatar actors to induce a broad range of responses in human subjects. By monitoring the speed and variability of heart rate, skin conductance responses, and the speed and tone of verbal responses, they concluded that avatars can substitute for real humans when studying responses in humans. In fact, they concluded that we humans respond realistically to virtual characters as if they're real—*even if we know they're not*. They write in their conclusion: "Our results show that in spite of the fact that all participants knew for sure that neither the stranger nor the shocks were real, the participants ... tended to respond to the situation at the subjective, behavioral, and physiological levels as if it were real."

These findings indicate that we understand our experiences when we're driving our avatar as "real."

In 1817, the British poet and literary critic Samuel Tayor Coleridge wrote in his book *Biographia Literaria*:

> "In this idea originated the plan of the "Lyrical Ballads"; in which it was agreed, that my endeavours should be directed to persons and characters supernatural, or at least romantic; yet so as to transfer from our inward nature a human interest and a semblance of truth sufficient to procure for these shadows of imagination that willing *suspension of disbelief* for the moment, which constitutes poetic faith."

We no longer only have lyrical ballads that create a suspension of disbelief, we now (if we believe the media equation) have "real" worlds in which "real" people are saying "real" things. Psychologically, the definition of "real" gets damn slippery. For a long time we were unable to enter into our stories. Now we inhabit and affect them in surprising ways. And now we share our narratives with others in online virtual environments.

Shared experiences create a sense of reality.

Experiences create a grounding of belief. People in virtual worlds build things, use them, sell them, trade them, and discuss them. When another person confirms what I'm seeing, places value on it, spends time working to pay for it, buys it, keeps it, uses it, talks about it, gets emotional about it, and then sells it—this tells me there is something real happening. The suspension of disbelief has become a grounding of belief. Avatar-driven systems confirm that what we thought we saw was, on some level, real. And that is enough for me (and millions of other people) to commit time, emotions, attention, reputation, and money.

But it is all based on the fact that we are sharing a narrative. It is all based on the notion that if I see something and someone else sees the same thing there is a "grounding of belief." In his fine book *Synthetic Worlds: The Business and Culture of Online Games*, Edward Castronova writes:

> "If everyone pretends the dragon is real, and reacts as though the dragon is real, then for that society it is real, just as real as the value of a dollar. Thus as a result of both internal and external costs, it becomes more mentally and socially expensive to disbelieve the dragon than to believe it."

So a virtual glass of wine above a virtual ocean shared with an avatar is as important to us, psychologically and socially, as a real glass of wine on a real cliff with a real friend.

Pighed Stonecutter and Montserrat Snakeankle sit together on a cliff
where they enjoy Gorean wine and something that is not a sunset.

Ceci n'est pas un coucher de soleil.

The Night of the Dance

My real life had space and time for this world. When I wasn't traveling somewhere I was living on my sailboat. I had few expenses and even less space and since I really wanted a large painting studio I was partly attracted to Second Life as an *atelier* where I could work on virtual paintings and sculpture. Having little space and few expenses also urged me to see if I could make a living as a builder and so, motivated more by want than need, I dedicated myself to the effort of learning to build, pick up some pocket change, and see what I could do artistically.

The months passed quickly. There was always a lot to do in-world, and so, outside, in the real world, the seasons began to change. Sometimes, in-world, while I was working on chairs or walls or making a little painting for someone's avatar's home, visitors would drop by Tenaya Spirals for a visit. I'd be working away, and one of the alarms I'd set up to notify me of visitors would ping. I'd stop work and turn around to greet whoever was dropping by my workshop. Generally, we discussed in-world events. Someone was upset because their neighbor had built a new high-rise and was selling advertising space that polluted the mountain view, or someone had built an entire village underwater, or other such trivia. These were fictions that people had acted out; fictions that had become, for our little community, strangely real.

As the definition of "real" got increasingly obscure, I generated a little smoke of my own from time to time. One day a friend of mine, Velvethorn, pointed out that I was shirtless. I explained that I had been standing around at the "seam" of the island, that edge of nowhere, where no avatar may travel (if you try you are simply unable to walk forward, as if a big glass plate were barring your progress). I said a frog-human had crawled out from under the island and said, "I would like your shirt." I gave it to him, and he disappeared into the seam of nonexistence.

When Velvethorn heard this she got excited. She told Sparrowhawk, who notified some of the Linden Lab employees who spend time in-world. The Lindens—the people who run Second Life and serve as a kind of all-knowing nobility—expressed some concern and said they would keep an eye out for this frog-human, who was obviously a hacker of some sort.

CAUTION: SHIRT-STEALING FROG WAS HERE (18 feb).

Three days later, two strangers told me frog-people were living under the islands of Second Life. My glee at hearing this could only have been exceeded by that of the person who invented the story about alligators living under New York City.

I must confess that no frog existed. Though I owned a couple of shirts, I never wore them. The frog was utter fiction on my part—I was simply interested in showing off my tattoos. But the story got people excited about the possibilities of an impossible world, and it got me excited about the fact that nothing was impossible when it came to interactive forms of narrative. The line between fiction and reality could be so easily blurred as to be nearly nonexistent. I was using my avatar to create more interactive fictions within the fiction of Shivar, within the fiction of Second Life.

The layers of fiction made things seem more real.

As Gertrude Stein might have done, Sparrowhawk decided that Tenaya Spirals was an art piece that required an unveiling. She hired a DJ and a lighting designer and invited a bunch of people to see my sculpture/home, which was quickly being transformed into a nightclub for the opening.

By hiring people, I mean she really paid them money. Not a lot, only about US$15 total, but still, it represented real money, and so their labor was a real thing too, and that's pretty important when you think about it. The fact that money is changing hands as a result of labor in what looks like a video game alters not only the definition of money but the definition of work, too. Yet it's been happening for a long time. People have been rendering non-tangible services for years: fortune tellers and financial advisors, lawyers and doctors, painters and (yes, dear reader) writers. The only difference was Second Life allowed a broader range of intangible services. After all, if one has a virtual head one needs a virtual hat.

I had never been to a virtual party before. It hadn't occurred to me that it would be possible.

First to come were my new pals Rraven Moonlight and Dezire Moonlight. I'd met them, by chance, while flying over their island, some days back. In real life they were Canadians named Richard and Rose. Dezire generally wore tight leather hot-pants and high spike heels. So would Rraven. They were both the spit-fire cybergoth sort, always tossing jokes and faking drama. But their lives were quite seriously connected to the system. While logged into Second Life, they played footsie under their table in Canada, chatted with people on the phone, built for fun, profit, and status, and spent the day managing their island—which was a huge mall, one of the more successful in Second Life. And they did this all night as well, going for days without sleeping. They were next to each other always, in both worlds. He had bad knees, she had a bad back, and neither could work or collect unemployment. Second Life gave them an *out*. And they were probably two of the most generous, kindest, and imaginative people I've ever had the luck to meet.

Next to appear was YadNi Monde, the celebrated Builder, driving a huge spider avatar. In real life YadNi was David, a hotel night clerk in Brittany, France. He was abrupt, skinny, and 38. YadNi built most of Shivar and had particular artistic ideas about it. He was probably the most accomplished Builder I'd met in Second Life. Working as a night clerk served his life as an avatar perfectly as he was making money in the real world, doing little at his desk other than greeting the occasional nightly guest, and meanwhile, in-world, leading a parallel existence.

aEoLeuS Waves was dressed up in a business suit and tie, with sparkly shoes, just like a normal business geek. He was selling virtual laptops for Dell. Uriel Harbringer teleported over, dressed in glorious red skin, black raven wings, and fascinating black chaps. She was carrying a large bow and snapped off arrows from time to time. Her partner, Travis Maeterlinck, was a well-traveled, well-known Fur and security expert decked in missile launchers, machine guns, armor, and little blinking lights. Hal Mendicant was there as well, a kind of playboy that from that night on gave me the creeps whenever he talked about women. He made a living in Second Life by selling soft-porn artwork.

The DJ, Korya Sieyes, showed up with 20 other avatars. We were all on the dance floor with live music and commentary streaming to our browsers. Korya was talking about how fabulous we all looked (or didn't), and our avatars were doing a dance step in time, like a huge vaudeville chorus line, and we were giggling about Gwen Stefani and showing off moves to each other and throwing clothes around and dancing on the furniture and making fools of ourselves. This is what one does at a dance, right?

I never got Korya's real name. As it turned out, she lived with Richard and Rose (Rraven and Dezire). They told me that they'd met her in Second Life. Evidently she'd had some serious problems with an abusive family and ran out into the Canadian winter. She would log into SL from various coffee shops and Internet cafes, make a little money, find some way to collect some change, but she had been basically living off the street. A few weeks later she had moved in with Richard and Rose, and they were helping get her on her feet again. She was applying for a job as a telephone help-desk person. As for her avatar, Korya was hot. White hot. A slyly pouty goth and a smart-ass attitude gets me hot, and there was something about the curves of her avatar that just seemed just right. The music was pumping, dancelights were swinging, we were laughing and smoking little cigarettes, and the stars twinkled gently above us as we shook our avatar booties.

And Korya was sexy as a mink.

At this point, dear reader, you might be thinking, "Oh, puh-lease. An avatar dance? An avatar crush? This is an *avatar* we're talking about. How could you be attracted to an avatar?" Well, as any *Playboy* photographer will tell you, realism has little to do with eroticism. It's all about the psychological symbols. An avatar, just like a photo, painting, or film, can turn you on. These psychological symbols and my feelings for them were another grounding for my belief in what was happening around me.

Avatar porn is nothing new.

Ask Francois Rabelais, Alberto Vargas, or Betty Page—pornography has always been about virtual sex. We're simply finding new ways to virtualize it. For example, caLLie cLine, a Second Life photographer and designer, was rated number 95 in the Hot 100 list of women in the May 2007 issue of *Maxim* magazine. Was a line crossed when this "photo" was published in the real world? This picture is one of many signs that avatars are becoming ready to step out into something closer to what we currently think of as "human."

caLLie cLine, Second Life

THE MORNING AFTER

In "reality" it was 8 a.m., and I was sitting in a small apartment above a canal in Holland. Outside the snow was gently falling on some ducks, which were huddled together from the cold. All I had in the fridge were a few pieces of waxy herring and some orange juice that had gone acidic days ago. And I was starting to shiver. Meanwhile, in Second Life, the party was winding down a bit. Korya and four others were still joking and dancing. It was 2 a.m. in Second Life, which is also to say that it was 2 a.m. where the Second Life servers were located, in Pacific Standard Time. Eventually, I logged out and after warming myself in the shower I went to sleep as the sun headed for early afternoon.

57

The next morning—I mean the next Second Life morning—my little virtual home depressed me. If you've ever had a wild party at your house, you know the feeling. It's that peculiar, exhaustion-induced, depressing feeling at all the cigarette butts and beer bottles, and I wasn't sure what to do with all the rigging and lights that had been set up. Delete them? Could I store them somewhere? But while I floated there above the post-party carnage, meditatively pulling at my chin, YadNi showed up.

"We need to move it," he abruptly said.

"Oh," I replied.

"Let's make it a permanent club."

"Oh. Uh, okay."

My stomach fell when I heard this. It was bad enough that I had been traveling so much in real life that I had focused on building a stupid little "home" in Second Life, and it was bad enough that this one home I had left had been turned into an ashtray, but to have my own little ashtray re-moved...and then feel bad about that? Well, it just made me feel worse, and then weird. But YadNi was a Builder, and I figured he knew best since he'd been here for over a year now, and I was just a lowercase visitor and doubted myself. So we went ahead and moved my home-club underneath the Big Castle, and the beach once again became just the beach.

I think YadNi meant well. His motive was to protect the design of Shivar, which had begun to attract visitors. He felt it was his responsibility to keep things in good aesthetic order.

Nearly a month passed. I spent what time I could in-world, depending on real-life demands. Usually the only thing that interrupted me was travel. Sometimes I'd get a commission or a consulting gig and that herded me into the real world. But generally I managed six or more hours a day.

I made little worlds. I built wine glasses, beer mugs, carpets, floating tables, curtains that moved, walls of water, stone cottages, cliffside dwellings, sprawling warehouses, offices with hidden doors, crumbling castles, forests of listening trees, hillsides with secret entrances, mountain ranges, entire islands that framed small cities, and created the myths and stories that glued these things together. I made avatar bodies (just the blank white mannequin), and skins, and clothes, and hair, and eyes, and fingernails, and wings, and jewelry. I modified

stuff I found: shoes that spoke, watches that listened, and modified big discs that lifted my friends and me up into the clouds for a secret rendezvous of artificially inflated importance.

Most of these building jobs were commissions. People paid me in Linden dollars—the in-world currency of Second Life—and I was able to have those moved over to my credit card, or Linden Lab would send me a check in the mail when I cashed them in. So it was play money that could be converted, just like regular credit on a car, or gold, or a gift certificate from a restaurant. Someone asked me to make a particular thing, such as an embroidered coat for a late-night, New York-style jazz dinner. Sometimes people just asked me to furnish a palace or build a cottage. I built a big Cheshire Cat for Rraven and Dezire (based on the design of a friend and fellow artist named American McGee) to attract more people to their shopping mall. Other times I would build a house for people, fill it with furniture, and sell it as an entire package. Build an island and fill it with buildings. Basically, I built whatever was needed and tended to specialize in finely crafted and slightly strange objects.

My work—and therefore my money—depended on my avatar.

My avatar was my reputation, my means of talking, my means of building and storing and buying and interfacing with this increasingly complex virtual world. But as an avatar, artist or not, these things I built were all just cultural commodities. Functioning in a virtual space is easy for artists: Virtual worlds are just pop culture, pop talent, pop imagination art galleries, places where cultural commodities are traded and sold because they hold social meaning. My reputation was more valuable to me than my work. It gave my work value. As my reputation grew, so did the demand for my work. And as the demand for my work grew, its value increased. My value. Without my reputation, I would not be referred for work and I could not be paid the virtual money that I converted into real money. Without it, I could not even have the credit that was needed to assure a potential patron that I could do the job that was needed. And that was all attached to my avatar.

Ultimately it became about how I made money—both in-world and in real life.

Various build jobs by Yours Truly

VIRTUAL WORK

The sun was setting off to my right, the ocean was whispering its repetitive secret off to my left, and I was finding new ways to weave together pixels, listening to music, having a cup of coffee, and enjoying my morning. It was actually evening in Second Life, morning in real life, and I was starting to lose track of my health. But it was okay; in the virtual world I was making a funky little chair, a woven-wood sort of sitter that had been commissioned by a distributor who specialized in ancient-style interior decoration. It would then be sold by a retailer in a shop on a nearby island for about US$0.40. Of course, people could also buy the same piece of furniture—the same software for it, I mean, as it was just an entry in a database—from me. The piece would be exactly the same either way, except they'd only have to pay me about a quarter. Once they bought it, they would place it in their home. Homes were for sale, too. Those cost about US$10.

Just as in the days of 1920s Southern California, there were a thousand get-rich-quick schemes.

Carmen's role or job, like Mary, the Santa Monica real-estate baron, was to lease real estate. Mine, like the developers that sold completely furnished houses in Culver City, was to sell completely furnished buildings. We had all been working hard lately, and Shivar Island was doing better financially. Just before the corporate smash appeared—an invasion of the corporations that both repelled and pleased us—our shops started picking up business, and the folks renting our space to sell their goods (shoes and so on) were making enough that the money ended

Blast Ferraris, Second Life

back in Sparrowhawk's pocket. The tier—that is, the amount required to cover rent—was US$200 per month. A few months previously, Sparrowhawk had been a bit stressed out about this. She hadn't been making as much money as she would have liked, of course. This was around at the same time she got canned from her well-paying real-life software job, and she and her sister decided to live together to take care of their ailing mother, and it was a few months before her dog had died. These real-life pressures had an effect on Carmen's second life, impacting her emotionally and therefore impacting her avatar, and what her avatar did, and that impacted how she ran the island of Shivar. And thus the real world began to encroach on our little magic kingdom.

Sparrowhawk had been told she could get rich doing this. Originally she thought this would happen by hosting weddings for a fee. That work amounted to providing the cathedral, some music, and the services necessary for the party, much as she later did for my own. She was told she could make about 2,000 dollars per wedding. Of course, when she was told this she had no idea what currency was being discussed—whether it was real U.S. dollars or virtual Linden dollars. She had thought she'd be able to pay the island's tier easily by renting out a few shops and doing a wedding or two a month. She realized her mistake the next day, when a friend did the math and pointed out she would need 20 or 30 shops. Not only would that be a huge headache, but the island would be a virtual strip-mall, without the green space she so wanted. So she took the tier on her own back. Fortunately, her tax accountant (her real-life tax accountant) informed her that a Schedule 525 would allow her costs in the virtual world to be tax-deductible.

> *Involving money in the equation of our little virtual world changed everything. Not because we were making money, but because we had invested our real lives.*

Ask anyone who bets on horses. Money can change a frivolous game into a mortally important question of social standing. The horse is an avatar of its owner. The arena is a virtual world where the owners interact, a theater that extends itself virtually to the millions who watch the race. These people put money in the pot, turning the horse into their avatar as well. But more than that, when they put that money in they put real-world status in the pocket of the owner. From a distance, we don't quite understand exactly what the horses are doing. They seem like avatars engaged in the odd ritual of chasing their tails: they bear strange names, they are dressed up and paraded about. But up close, when we see the money changing hands and see the other representations of social standing (the box seat sizes, the food consumed, the appearances of the high rollers with their hats and cigars), we begin to notice something more subtle.

The money changes the game into a measurement of real-world status.

The more money you put in, the more social standing you get back. *If* you win. Of course, the higher the stakes, the higher the visibility of failure, until, finally, at events like the Kentucky Derby there are huge primes put on horses that most Arabian kings wouldn't pay. But the money isn't really the important part.

It's just there to offer a method of measurement of gain and loss of social status. In a game, social currencies and monetary currencies are often interchangeable. This is the case in Gaia, Second Life, Eve Online, World of Warcraft, and many others. Players can literally buy social standing by paying groups such as Peons for Hire to put people to work leveling up a character, mining gold, hunting, selling objects, auctioning real estate, or acquiring *rares* (objects that have intense social or utilitarian value, but are rarely seen in-game).

It had been nearly a year since Carmen had begun to earn money in Second Life, and after a slow ramp-up business was picking up, foot traffic was increasing, and the fragile fabric of our little village's commerce was sewing itself together. We needed to keep the momentum going by growing our reputation as a place where business could be done and goods could be sold.

We were getting there. We had a solid crew selling interesting items. Rraven's shop sold eyeballs and hair. There was my art gallery, where I sold paintings, and Dezire's shoe store, and YadNi's miscellaneous utilities and furnishings shop. Vindi Vindaloo sold high-fashion Euro clothes, and Alexis Paw sold biker-style clothing. Saajuk Bogomil sold avatar bodies in odd machine shapes. And there was other stuff, most of it also for avatars: French fashion clothing, furniture, pinup girlie posters, gloves, hats, poses, and animations. There were around 200 avatar citizens on Shivar Island, and I felt, as one of its official "rulers," a certain need to help keep things rolling. And roll they did. Although we were not making bank, we were almost making enough to cover costs. It was, at least, proof of the possible.

At first we thought it was real estate that would be the big sales item because people needed it to sell avatar goods. The top sellers, the big-dollar items, were islands and large tracts of land, and they were the items everyone was discussing. This was back in 2005. The year before, an avatar named Zachurm "Death-ifier" Emegen, paid US$26,500 for his virtual island, which was at the time the highest price ever paid for a virtual item. He recouped the investment within a year. But in fact most of the money did not come from land and large transactions. Small, individual transactions made up the bulk of in-world sales, most of which were related to avatar accessories such as shoes, shirts, and eyeballs. The folks managing the shops were making about 70 percent of their revenues from these items. This meant that the majority of the money passed up the line came from the same kind of, shall we say, industry. Shivar Island was an indicator of a larger trend. Second Life and many other online social environments earn about 70 percent of their revenues from avatar-based goods. The large majority of user spending is avatar-based. For example Puzzle Pirates earns about 20 percent of their revenues from clothing, and another 35 percent from badges, with an additional 15 percent on miscellaneous goods that relate to either social decoration or game-based rules.

Two paychecks from Second Life; one for each world.

Avatar accessories can be divided into two groups. In game worlds, such as World of Warcraft or Eve Online, accessories are usually utilities, things that help achieve goals and maximize what liberty the rules offer. But in social worlds, like Second Life and Gaia, the primary accessories are decorative, things that help achieve social status and maximize the relationships with other avatars. It gradually became clear to us that the avatar was the fulcrum for finances in virtual worlds. Not until we stopped thinking of the island as an island and began to see it as a group of people did we realize where the financial value lay. After all, the island had a purpose, and it wasn't to divide the water. It was to group the avatars.

As for what it cost me to be in-world, my account was free, at least for the first year or so. The question was how to pay for the real-world needs—food, rent, clothes, and so forth. The money I made in SL came mostly from commissions, and with that I managed to cover about half of my daily living costs. I sold whatever people asked for. Chairs? Sure. Clothes? No problem. Paintings? Absolutely. I could make everything from castles to gloves to hands. For me it was artwork, and it was mostly fun. Some mornings, while drinking coffee and listening to music and inventing some new sculpture, I would realize that my second life had made working in a real-world corporate office an unthinkable nightmare. A nine-to-five schedule in a corporation of frigid politics became an increasingly distant threat; commuting, a misdemeanor; and a boss, a joke. Sure, I had to work hard, but at least I was enjoying what I did and at least it was work that gave me energy.

I saved my first L$100K and then cashed it out (I think it was worth around US$280, depending on the value of the Linden dollar). As in the real world, saving money was not always easy to do because often I'd want to buy a new virtual suit or a set of building tools. But this virtual money that I converted into U.S. dollars had real value for me each time I cashed it out. Oddly it became more valuable than dollars for me.

It's important to note that I lived, in the real world, quite simply. I lived on a sailboat, and it cost very little. Thus there was something satisfying about cashing in credits in Second Life and having them appear as a dinghy, or a windlass on the foredeck.

Blast Ferraris,
Second Life

Anshe Chung on the cover of
BusinessWeek, May 2006

THE SUITS COMETH

Meanwhile, established businesses were going nuts over virtual worlds, and Second Life in particular. In May 2006, an avatar appeared on the cover of *BusinessWeek* magazine.

It was Anshe Chung, also known in the real world as Ailin Graef, a woman who had multiple avatars in multiple game and social worlds. In SL, Anshe started with US$9.95. She began work as a fashion designer and graduated to prostitute, one who was a good enough writer to satisfy her sometimes high-profile clients. Then, once she'd squirreled away some L$, she cashed it out and sent it to the Philippines to support children there. Once she made more money she moved into the more respectable world of real estate. As the value of land in Second Life increased, she earned more than US$100,000 in 2006 and, according to Second Life press releases, had accumulated more than L$1,000,000 worth of in-world assets. She also invested US$60,000 in a banking license in Entropia Universe, another virtual world much like Second Life.

It was roughly three months after her avatar appeared on the *BusinessWeek* cover that boatloads of corporate voyagers began crashing upon the shores of Second Life, spilling out their unwashed masses to stagger around and orient themselves in this world. It was like a perverse Ellis Island. By April of 2007, Microsoft, MTV, NBC, AOL, BBC Radio, CNET, Vodafone, Fox, Reuters, Sony, *Popular Science*, and *Playboy* all had some representation in Second Life. That is to say, they all had places—they set up shops. Mercedes-Benz, Nissan, Pontiac, Toyota, and BMW soon followed. But it wasn't just the car and media companies; the hardware guys were flocking too: AMD, Cisco, Sun Microsystems, Dell, and

Philips all dealt themselves into the game. (IBM was famously rumored to have put in more than US$10,000,000. When I visited the small island IBM had built, I was surprised at how little had been done with so much; Roo Reynolds later informed me that the SL investment numbers had been greatly exaggerated.)

The hardware guys were quickly joined by manufacturers of softer goods: Sears, Adidas, American Apparel, Reebok, and Jean-Paul Gaultier.

These companies herded in, built islands, made little shops on the islands, and piled little virtual shirts and shoes and cars and laptop computers on the virtual shelves for sale. Then they logged out and watched the news and thought, "If you build it, they will come."

Evidently they thought they were still selling products to humans. But they weren't—they were selling to avatars. And that's a different market with different needs, desires, and fashion sense. After all, a Jean-Paul Gaultier shirt isn't so interesting when you're used to wearing a jet pack.

A year or so after the Anshe Chung *BusinessWeek* ran, Allison Fass of Forbes.com wrote an article titled, "Sex, Pranks, and Reality." In it she concluded that Second Life was not a healthy place for business. The article finished with a quote from Erik Hauser, creative director of Swivel Media, Wells Fargo's agency: "Going into Second Life now is the equivalent of running a field marketing program in Iraq."

Wired, the *Los Angeles Times*, and many others offered similar reports that cooled the hype of the year before: Business in virtual worlds is not what we had expected it would be, and we're not making money here.

Of course not.

If businesses do not understand how to make money in virtual worlds, it is usually because they are not paying attention to what is immediately in front of them—the avatar.

The avatar is the most overlooked
and undervalued asset on the Internet.

Most money in virtual worlds is made because of avatars. The value of all virtual goods, and the reasons for the sale of all virtual goods, orbit and link to the avatar. Here's why. First, virtual worlds are made of three components: architecture, object, and avatar. The architecture, or space, of the environment includes the stars, the sky, mountains and dales, buildings of all sorts, pathways, columns, plazas, piazzas, underground dungeons, and the tombs where the gold is buried. Architecture bounds space and defines place. It ropes off the virtual playing fields of imagined spaces. Functionally, architecture is used to frame story metaphor and avatar interaction. A continent in Entropia Universe or an island in Second Life is of no value if there are no avatars there. The spaces are there, literally, to support the interaction between avatars. Second, the object is what is contained in the architecture. *Objects* are things that include the trees and grass, the chairs and tables, the guns and bling, and in short anything that you can't fit your avatar into. Functionally, objects are like architecture; they exist to build the story metaphor and avatar interaction. They are there to define what avatars do, and why. But they're small and are commonly carried or contained. Finally, the avatar exists between the architecture and the objects. The architecture and the objects form two boundaries of reality: inside and outside. In a virtual world, whether it's for games or for social interaction, everything is designed for the avatar. The shirts and shorts, the guns and goggles, the building itself (roof, walls, and all), the mutants in the backyard, and the very ground it all rests upon is there to bring value and centralize the world around the avatar.

Another reason why the avatar is the center of virtual worlds is the fact that on the other side of the screen, the keyboard is connected to the user. The user is connected to the wallet. And the wallet is connected to the money the avatar is spending. Nothing, then, is more valuable than the avatar. In a virtual-world setting, the avatar holds the coin. Like McDonald's marketing to kids who in turn market to their parents, the avatar is the customer who gets marketed to.

Avatars are responsible for the community, for the commerce, and for the creation of content. Without these three things, the value to business guys is lost.

Selling something to an avatar is similar to selling something to a person. You need to know what it is they want, and why. The sense of personal interaction, the process of discovery and surprise, and the personal conviction that what they are doing will be good later on—for their avatar—is what makes the driver of that avatar decide to go ahead and grab the wallet.

The avatar is a specific persona, and different identity, of the driver.

But at the same time, selling something to an avatar is also quite different. An avatar has a different psychographic than its human driver; an avatar has different interests, because the avatar has different needs. Avatars don't use the same media and they don't watch the same television shows. People behave differently as their avatar and have different desires, different wants, and generally express a different persona. Avatars are interested in things that their driver may or may not be interested in. For example, three of my different avatars have slaughtered ogres, hit warp drive between galaxies, and bought levitation devices—all of which I have never done in real life. While buying the levitation device, my avatar had on Gene Simmons-style, high-tooth platform shoes—which I have never worn in the real world. So we are different, my avatar and I. This means that an avatar has a different demographic than its human driver.

This seems to be very confusing for business types. In most professional conversations within and around the virtual-worlds industry there is conflict and confusion to do with the terms *users, residents, subscribers, avatars*, and *players*. How many are there? What do they want? When are they logging in? For how long? Why? And so on. The confusion sits squarely on the border where the driver ends and the avatar begins, and it occurs because the presence in the virtual world is owned by the avatar, but the money in the real world is owned by the driver.

Part of the problem with this topic has to do with the precedent that was set in which a person driving an avatar is a "subscriber" or "resident" and is therefore constantly present. But product and service companies generally do not work with constantly present human users. People occasionally arrive, and then only for a short time, to complete the demand of the service provided. Avatars, like people, vary in their behavior. Think of an avatar as a person visiting a store: Some represent more value to a business than others because they have more money; some show up frequently because they place high value on replenishing what they're buying; some come at regular intervals because they have subscribed to a service; some are loyal customers who spread the brand propaganda; some identify with what is being sold; some feel and think and know what the marketers say they do.

What matters is not the population of people, but the population of avatars. In terms of everything that has value in a virtual world, it doesn't matter if I'm Korean or American. What matters is whether my avatar is from Entropia Universe or Second Life. That's the demographic that counts. Consider two avatars: One is an avatar driven by a 14-year-old girl in Seoul, and the other is driven by a 50-year-old man in New York. We might think that the Korean girl, should we generalize, will buy more bling for her avatar. But this is not necessarily the case. I have met a number of avatars who were driven by someone of the opposite gender. I have done it myself. One cannot say with due certainty that an avatar will have the same interests or attractions that the driver has.

On another, more interesting level, these businesses got confused because virtual worlds—especially Second Life—are all about rules and roles. Virtual worlds are interactive narratives, and the avatars are actors in a kind of street theater where the audience helps improvise the plot. If a salesman walked up to a small troupe of people dressed up and acting oddly in the middle of the street and asked them if they wanted to buy a car, and they ignored him, would it be clear why? No. The whole thing is like a joke, "A salesman walks into a bar and finds a rhino in a tutu talking dirty to the parrot on his shoulder...."

Understandably, you would be confused, too.

As Wagner James Au, a well-respected magnifying glass of emerging cultures, particularly Second Life, puts it: "...corporations must first come to a humbling realization: In the context of the fantastic, their brands as they exist in the real world are boring, banal, and unimaginative."

This seems important to note for the approximately one million companies that rely on the Internet economy for more than 50 percent of their revenues. After all, as we've discussed, an avatar is not necessarily one that exists in a 3-D environment.

Presto Merlin, Second Life

How Avatars Affect the Real World

Big Business was storming Second Life and coming up short, but many of us unattached to corporations were making money in Second Life and from other systems as well, such as World of Warcraft, Eve Online, Entropia Universe, and others. Though many lived in the United States, I knew a couple of Koreans that were getting by as clothing designers, YadNi the Builder seemed to be making at least as much as David the hotel clerk was, and though Rraven and Dezire were on the edge, they didn't fall off it.

All of us were, effectually, creating money and moving it into the countries we were living in, whether it was the U.S., Korea, Canada, or France. We were actually importing money into our countries, as if bringing gold from another continent. And I suppose it was when the U.S. Joint Economics Committee began to rally a call that in-world developers pay taxes that I realized the impact we were having. Fortunately, Julian Dibbell had written a piece about virtual taxation and interactions with the IRS, which got into the hands of Congressional Economist Dan Miller. Miller wanted to do a report on the phenomenon which would show why it was a bad idea, nipping off efforts by the IRS, or other government actors, before things really bloomed. From in-world, it's worth noting that the response among those of us that were producing goods was quite negative. It's not that we mind paying taxes if we get something in return. But why pay taxes to a government that is neither developing nor supporting your infrastructure? What, really, is the benefit to the tax payer?

Castronova, in *Synthetic Worlds*, cites three important events that occur once a user has crossed the hurdle of entry into virtual worlds. The first is when the avatar's attributes feel like they are your own personal attributes. The second is when you have an emotional investment in an event in the virtual world. The third is when you recognize that labor in a virtual world can be valued just like labor in the real world—that virtual money is money and that a virtual world is still a world. He goes on to extend his argument, pointing out that a synthetic world can, in principle, affect macroeconomic conditions on earth. But Castronova stops short, in my opinion. I'd like to drag his argument over the edge with me. Avatars affect much more than the macroeconomic conditions that surround us, and on multiple levels.

In 2007, The Maldives was the first country to open an embassy in Second Life, and it was followed shortly by Sweden. In January of that year, avatar supporters of Jean-Marie Le Pen, a far-right French politician, created small-scale skirmishes on the Second Life island of Porcupine, a relatively nondescript shopping island. Real-life politicians Nicolas Sarkozy and Ségolene Royal made appearances as avatars in Second Life as they were running for the French presidency. Their presence indicated that there is a message to be spread, and spending time in a virtual world is a means of doing so. Though I find the Le Pen backers are more interesting (because they're there all the time), Barack Obama and Hillary Clinton have also made appearances in Second Life and other systems as well, such as Facebook and MySpace. This is to say nothing of the social impact that these systems have had on people like Rudy Giuliani, as he also runs for the presidency of the United States; and his daughter's opinions, which she posted on Facebook, make headlines. And on the other side of the coin, in September 2005, Second Life residents pooled money and sent aid to victims of Hurricane Katrina.

Avatars are affecting financial markets and are introducing new ones. In May 2007, in the virtual world of Entropia Universe, the world's first virtual banking licenses were auctioned for a total of US$404,000 to a consortium of real-world banks, Entropia Universe celebrities, and entrepreneurs. The five banking licenses allow for avatar services, just as you might expect any bank to offer. They allow the lending of money, the building of new banks, advertisers, and provides for other avatar-to-avatar services. About two weeks after this, it was announced that the Chinese government was working with Entropia Universe (via Cyber Recreation Development, or CRD) to create a cash-based virtual economy for China. The partnership is expected to generate US$1 billion annually in avatar-generated commerce and produce 10,000 new jobs. As of August 2007, the total GDP of virtual worlds is estimated to be around US$28.15 billion. According to the World Bank and the International Monetary Fund, that puts it the upper third of all countries on the planet—a little richer than Sri Lanka and about as wealthy as Lithuania.

Avatars are affecting education. According to a 2007 *New York Times* article, more than 100 Second Life islands have been sold for educational purposes. Some of the buyers include Harvard, Stanford, Vassar, Pepperdine, Rice, University College Dublin, New York University, and the Australian Film Television and Radio School. Lawrence Lessig, Noam Chomsky, and other well-known educators have made guest appearances in Second Life, in old-school, Socratic-style presentations. The Kuurian Expedition is sponsored by the Synthetic Worlds Initiative at Indiana University. Its research has uncovered far more shocking things than anyone this writer personally knows.

Avatars are also affecting religion. Antonio Spadaro, a Jesuit academic, wrote in the Rome-based journal *La Civilta Cattolica*, "Deep down, the digital world can be considered, in its way, mission territory. Second Life is somewhere where the opportunity to meet people and to grow should not be missed." In late 2005, a female avatar named Palemoon Twilight and her in-world husband (her real-life fiancé, whom she met in Second Life) Lumpy Tapioca founded what may well be the first every-Sunday church service in Second Life. The Unitarian Universalist Association has a "church" of sorts in Second Life as well, on the island of Modest.

Avatars are affecting science. In June of 2007, Richard Dawkins, the pope of atheism and inventor of the *meme* meme, was interviewed in Second Life by well-known in-world reporter Wagner James Au. Au asked Dawkins about observing evolutionary trends in Second Life and Dawkins replied, "I think that certainly there's very scientific research you could do in Second Life…. I mean sociological research, psychological research, it could be very interesting. I suppose you could imagine some science fiction scenario in the distant future when people live in SL so much that they hardly even know there is an outside world and it becomes a matter of theological speculation of what goes on in the outside world." Dr. William Bainbridge, head of Human-Centered Computing at the U.S. National Science Foundation, has recognized that people respond to virtual worlds in the same way we do the real world and now uses that to guide scientific research. In *Science* magazine, he noted that social scientists are coming to prefer conducting their social research in virtual worlds for a number of reasons, ranging from being able to easily find more subjects to administering broader tests to being able to collect deeper data.

Avatars are affecting families. Family-law experts are seeing an increasing number of marriages dissolve over virtual infidelity. Officially, legally, online flings don't count as adultery until they cross over into the real world, but these virtual romps are being cited as grounds for divorce. Moreover, they could be a factor in determining alimony and child custody in some states, according to several legal experts. One such expert is Jeff Atkinson, author of the American Bar Association's book *Guide to Marriage, Divorce and Families* and a professor at DePaul University College of Law. Another is Kimberly Young, founder of the Center for Internet Addiction Recovery and a clinical psychologist. She handles more than 200 counseling cases a year, and the majority of them involve fantasy role-playing games. "They start forming attachments to other players," she says. "They start shutting out their primary relationships." But let's not get too far out there. Avatars are fun for the whole family, too. According to

The Entertainment Software Association, thirty-five percent of American parents say they play computer and video games, and 80 percent of them play games with their kids. Two-thirds of them said that playing games has brought their family closer together.

Avatars are also affecting new, synthetic families. You may remember that in their real lives Rraven and Dezire gave Korya, whom they met in Second Life, a place to live. Shortly after Korya moved in, while Rraven and Dezire were out of the house one day, Korya stole family jewelry, computer equipment, credit cards, some clothing—and the sense of pride they had received from her getting back on her feet.

Avatars are affecting the environment. In a now-famous 2005 essay, Nicholas G. Carr (http://www.roughtype.com/) calculates that the average Second Life avatar consumes 1,752 kilowatt hours per year, not far behind the average human worldwide, who consumes 2,436 kWh per year. Carr points out that this is roughly equivalent to the amount of energy a Brazilian uses. In a related essay, Sun Microsystem's Dave Douglas uses a calculation of carbon dioxide emissions. He writes, "… looking at CO2 production, 1,752 kWh/year per avatar is about 1.17 tons of CO2. That's the equivalent of driving an SUV around 2,300 miles (or a Prius around 4,000)."

Strategy Analytics, a technology and business research organization, released a report in September 2007 titled "Online Games: Global Market Forecast" in which they estimate there are 30 million total subscriptions across all MMORPGs, with 73 percent coming from the Asia-Pacific region. Much of what this book claims and predicts, therefore, hinges on decisions that will come from that region of the world.

Presto Merlin, Second Life

71

Happiness Is a Warm Gun

Real-world impacts are useful to note, but the main thing avatars are good for is practicing for real life. Consider how puppies play. It looks like they're fighting. They bite each other on the neck and stand on one another and make noises that, if magnified to adult levels and bumped up a speed cycle or two, would start to sound pretty dangerous. In a game, the bets are on, but the stakes are low. Puppies are simply learning to fight and they both know it on some level. Avatars work this way, too. An avatar can be seen as a rehearsal mechanism we can use to figure out the important stuff in real life.

It was morning, and I was at my cliffside home above the sea, working on my chairs. Shivar was doing well, and we all wanted to keep it that way. We were all working to see that the little economic bubble we had made didn't pop. Suddenly, my screen went blank. My health meter, the little indicator of my overall health, dropped to zero. Then the screen lit up again and I reappeared at my home location. I didn't know that I had died, but as I figured out what had happened, I got a message from Sparrowhawk saying that she had been shot, too. Then another message came in: Mortain had been shot. Then Sparrowhawk was shot again, and then someone shopping at the mall got it. Then the rat bastard shot me again and then shot the Queen a third time. All in probably less than two minutes.

My pulse started to race. In the real world, I've visited three war zones and know what it is to be shot at. This was quite similar. And I was being shot at in my own home, meaning retaliation was a requisite. Fortunately, I had a weapon I'd been using for target practice, but it was a staff that threw hot sparks, and I knew I couldn't handle whoever it was that was shooting us. I called in reinforcements, and they called in the cavalry, and soon Shivar Island was a beehive astir as eight of us flew around the spires of the town, shooting whatever weird weapons we had found or made.

But not me; I wasn't physically coordinated enough. I had learned skills for making chairs, not throwing lightning bolts. I knew enough to know what to do, but all my shots were off, whereas this fellow, dressed in black with a helmet and a jetpack, was an unerring shot and was picking us off every second or two.

Eventually, I got a lucky shot in, and he disappeared, teleported back to his home island. But before he did, I got his name: Killingmachine Marx.

We were all a little upset by this. Imagine someone coming into your home and kicking your cat, hard. Something had to be done. I dedicated the rest of the day to long-range target practice. I needed coordination and better weapons. I needed a solid offense and a decent defense. I didn't know what weapons were needed but I knew I needed them—a shield, maybe, and a gun. And practice. I needed to change myself, and I needed to do it fast. He would probably come back, but even if he didn't, my pride was still bleeding.

What this called for was, quite literally, new arms. If you can imagine your arms as guns, that is what was needed. But what I found on the Second Life black market were a cranial implant, a tracking device, alert systems—and a new avatar. It was a gnat-sized body I could climb into, designed specifically for shooting and being shot at, and it even fired 100-percent accurate, heat-seeking missiles. While I practiced, I remembered my days on AOL, the days of trolling and collecting enemies, a bit bored, not much else to do, and it finally occurred to me how stupid I was being. One does not shoot at an enemy. One must be cleverer than that. I schemed and thought out a new plan that wouldn't require bullets and gnat-sized avatars. Then I sent Sparrowhawk a message.

The next morning, after some strategy discussion, Sparrowhawk and I called in the five most baddest-assed folks we knew, armed to the teeth, and determined to protect the island.

I sent Killingmachine Marx an instant message.

"I'm the guy that zapped you yesterday. Why not come back and we'll have a legitimate challenge for you to deal with?"

Of course he appeared, and as soon as he did I used one of my new, slightly illegal tools to trap him under a tall glass cylinder, like a fly in a jar. He couldn't shoot or fly. He couldn't do much of anything other than talk and listen.

We gathered around him on the bridge and finally got a good look at him. Dressed in grey and black camouflage, Killingmachine Marx was clearly designed for one thing: killing. He had steel fingers and a priest-like collar that gave his oxygen mask a hollow skull-like appearance. Great avatar.

While Bear floated overhead, I sat down on the railing. YadNi and Saajuk stood nearby listening in. Sparrowhawk glided up, decked out in full courtly regalia: long green queenie dress, sparkly little tiara, and even white gloves. Following is a snippet from my chat log:

Sparrowhawk Perhaps: "As queen of Shivar I forbid you to plague my peaceful people here. We are quiet, but when enraged, dangerous. You are forbidden to kill here. However, if you would like, we have a position in our military for a person with your skills."

YadNi Monde: "Where did you come from? What are you doing here?"

Killingmachine was quiet.

Sparrowhawk Perhaps: "If you deign to join us we will provide you with a stipend and a home of your choosing. Does this interest you?"

Killingmachine was still quiet.

Pighed Stonecutter: "Aw, come on, Killer, we're making you one helluva good offer here."

Killingmachine Marx: "Ok ."

Rraven Moonlight: "A man of many words."

Sparrowhawk Perhaps: "Very well then. You will be assigned a home and a position in the military. You are, however, not allowed to kill on other islands under the name of the Shivar Tribe. Is that understood?"

Killingmachine Marx: "Ok."

That was that. He had a new role to play, a new life to lead, free of sin. I imagined Killingmachine getting a little portly in the coming months, lounging around the hills of Shivar with not too much killing to do, a retiree from his earlier days of hunting strangers for amusement.

He and I flew up to an upper hillside, and I asked him what he wanted by way of a home. His answer was "a bunker," of course. So we built an ice-cave bunker together and talked a little bit. After that, from time to time we would trade a few words here and there, but for the most part he was off on other islands, probably killing people.

Because there wasn't much killing to do around Shivar Island, he eventually stopped showing up. We were pretty lame merchants and artists, I guess. But as I learned over the course of the week, Killingmachine was, in the real world, a German guy who didn't really speak English. And as any video game designer can tell you, if you can't talk you end up resorting to simpler interactions. And the simplest interaction known to man is killing.

Zhin Murakami, Second Life

75

A Few Notes on Griefing and Morality

Part of what Killingmachine Marx was doing, in showing up on our island and shooting us, was called *griefing*. This is behavior that is intended, simply, to cause grief. When characters are engaged in peaceful interactions, and a non-contextual interaction (usually violent) gets plopped into the middle of the scene, it's usually griefing.

World of Warcraft saw a famously controversial instance of griefing one day in early March of 2006. The week before, a popular player had died from a real heart attack, and approximately 40 of her in-world friends held a ceremony for her next to a virtual lake in a part of World of Warcraft named Winterspring. Her boyfriend logged in to her account, and the group carried her deathly still avatar to the lakeside and formed a large circle around it to perform the remembrance ceremony. While all eyes were on her boyfriend, who was reciting final rites, a member from a rival guild walked up and attacked him in plain sight, unprovoked. It was a funeral ambush led by a group named Serenity Now, and it sparked months of online discussion around griefing. Some saw it as barbaric and insensitive to the funeral goers, arguing the in-world ceremonies need to be respected. Others simply pointed out the funeral was held on contested land.

The Winterspring funeral goers argued that holding a funeral in a social environment is natural and warranted and that attacking them had been tasteless and inappropriate. Serenity Now retorted that attacks are warranted and natural and that funerals are tasteless and inappropriate. Both arguments rest on the same premise: There is precious little distance between driver emotions and avatar actions. In other words, the avatars of Serenity Now acted out the emotions of their real-world users. Serenity Now was doing the same thing they were complaining about; they just used a different ritual while doing it. Whether the killing or the funeral is more valuable is the core of the debate, because virtual killing and real-world funerals are both well-respected rituals in World of Warcraft.

Avatars find odd and inventive ways to play with the system. In June 2006, Cally, an avatar in Eve Online, opened a bank with some other avatars and began collecting investments. Avatars deposited money with the hope of gaining interest from investments the bank made. By August Cally had accumulated more than ISK700 billion (InterStellar Kredits, worth approximately US$170,000). Cally faked his own in-game death and logged off. The ISK, like the Linden Dollar, is an in-world currency, having no real-world value unless it is cashed out, and because Cally didn't technically go against the Eve Online End User's License Agreement (EULA) he didn't, technically, commit a crime. In fact, because he didn't violate the agreement, he might even be given another avatar.

This wasn't the first time such a thing had happened in Eve. In 2004, Eve Online avatar Dentara Rask called Eve "a poorly designed game which rewards the greedy and violent, and punishes the hardworking and honest." He was referring to the game dynamics that made it easier to play a pirate and harder to play a merchant. To prove the truth of his statement, he and other players did the same thing Cally ended up doing, except Dentara Rask's motives were not personal profit but the punishment of CCP games (or Crown Control Productions), the Icelandic company that started Eve Online.

The issue is, again, moral. What rituals are appropriate when? What importance do we put on these interactions? What is the significance of an avatar's death versus a real person's death? What do our avatars do that are a result of our emotions? What is the importance of play money? When is it appropriate to draw a line between real and virtual?

WANTED
DEAD OR ALIVE

Suspect is wanted in connection with the theft of 700 billion ISK. If you have any information regarding their whereabouts please contact your local authorities.

http://techfilter.net/photos/cally.gif

Cally
Eve Online

It's been argued (by Mark Wallace and others who post about these moral questions) that griefing is just another kind of play, and that Killingmachine Marx or the Winterspring funeral slaughter were both just new and inventive ways for people to play. But I mention griefing here not because of how it applies to social structures, but because it is also a part of what an avatar, intrinsically, is—a device for social fictions, for ritual, and for the re-invention of ritual. It is a device for archetype. It is a self-discovery process. Fritz Pearles, the famous gestalt therapist, used to ask people to play roles to bring out aspects of themselves or other personalities. By externalizing, Pearles' client was able to relate to and see other personalities in a new context. It could be argued that griefing does much the same thing.

Griefing helps establish morality. How power is used determines, to a large degree, what laws become passed. It has always been the classic griefers—Captain Cook, Jesse James, Bonnie and Clyde—who cause a complete rethink of society's rules. These people caused great grief by living at the edges of the rules, and the avatars we see today, blowing up financial schemes, raiding funerals, and raining bullets on virtual islands will be the ones that influence the "law" more than the chair-makers and slaves.

We are using avatars to test new moralities, to test the ideas of old moralities, and to test the possibilities of worlds in which no such thing as morals exist.

In two separate polls
I asked 300 people
the same question:

"Can sin be committed
via your avatar?"

150 people said yes, 150 said no.

78

Falcon Nacon's Slave Kit

79

GUNID'S BABIES

Note: "The story you are about to hear is true. Only the names have been changed to protect the innocent."

Gunid Sorky's breasts were too big. And she typed too slowly. And she was a psycho about babies. I was certain that she was either a teenager or a Russian, but I couldn't decide which. I wasn't sure if I trusted her, but I had no reason not to. Gunid was Sparrowhawk's administrative assistant on Shivar, making about \$L2000 per month, or around US\$5. She had two jobs, and she danced when she wasn't playing secretary to Sparrowhawk.

Gunid got pregnant. In order to "get pregnant," you bought a script (or your lover bought it for you) and dragged it onto your avatar. Ham sandwiches and Chinese food came with it. Over the coming weeks, you ended up with a belly and eventually had a thing called a *prim baby*. Prim babies came in four different shapes, one for each week of the four-week pregnancy. They cost roughly \$L4000 (around US\$10). Once it was born, every few minutes you got a message about how the baby was moving, or a whisper, something like "Mommy I love you" or "Hungry now." You didn't have to be female to get pregnant. It was an equal opportunity oddity. YadNi was pregnant for several minutes by a sea horse, though he never had the kid.

Sparrowhawk also got pregnant somehow, though nobody was sure by whom. Her baby died while we were standing on the beach, so we had to bury it. We buried it underwater in a 30-second memorial service, near the grave of Sparrowhawk's former self. Gunid was the saddest of us all and it wasn't even her baby. Hell, it wasn't even a baby.

Gunid's ninth pregnancy was with Hal Mendicant. It was Gunid who decided she was pregnant, and though Hal was relatively easygoing about the situation, by week three they had broken up. Gunid chose to carry the baby to term anyway. When the baby was "born," it was clearly a piece of fiction, clearly a prim baby, an icon in a virtual world, Hal, reasonably enough, never asked how "the baby" was doing. Gunid came at it from a different angle, though. She was a bit concerned that Hal didn't ask about it. She thought he might not care about it, or might not recognize his responsibilities as a father. Sparrowhawk communicated this to Hal:

Sparrowhawk Perhaps: "Gunid is a little worried for the baby."

Perhaps 10 or 15 seconds passed. Hal: "She does know its a *prim* baby, doesn't she?"

Sparrowhawk: "Yes, it's not a real baby."

Hal: "I know that. I hate to say this, but I really feel like I need to say she may need professional help."

Last I heard, Gunid wouldn't talk to Hal since he had abandoned their child. But she had other husbands, some of whom had children in the real world. Currently, Gunid has at least eleven prim babies by at least five fathers, one of whom is a Furry. She wants to find people in the real world who will role play these babies for her and in fact says she'll pay the actor to do this work. Once upon a time, she sent me the job descriptions.

Olyana Rana Sorky-Rebel—10months old.
    She is a quiet little girl,
    but always knows what she wants.

Sunny Angel Sorky-Rebel—8months old.
    Quiet, but is some what adventurous.

Dawn Sunny Rebel-Sorky—7months old.
    She is my most active child.

Pokea Rebel-Sorky—6months old.
    She never knew her father, but
    thinks she is mommy's favorite.

Niofa Sorky-Mendicant—3months old.
    My smallest child, feels resentment
    after her father wanted no interest in her.

Fait and Hophe Nosferatu-Sorky—1 month old.
    My beautiful twins, bounded by blood;
    are a team they must get what they want.

    In fact, there were "baby clinics" where actors could find baby-portrayal work on request boards, so this might not have been so uncommon. But on the other hand, maybe Hal was right. Maybe Gunid, with an imagination that powerful, needed help from someone.

    Then again, maybe we all do. I have done strange things in my virtual life. Many people specifically go into Second Life to do strange things—things they cannot do in their first life. How, finally, is Gunid any different from the avatar who has 58 pairs of shoes? How is she different from the avatar who spends enormous amounts of time and money lavishly furnishing five mansions, delicately trimming the shrubbery in the front yard, fastidiously focusing on the hem of a skirt, or the pixel on an eyebrow? What it indicates to me is Gunid, or whoever was driving Gunid, was someone who knew how to use the system to full advantage. None of us knows, finally, what others need.

WHY?

My second life was much like my first, only accelerated, smaller, and more dramatic. People married, money moved, wars began, kingdoms crumbled. Noses and lips and hair and clothes shifted like tiny weather systems, raining images and emotions onto the computer screens of people around the world. Little programs that animated your avatar to kiss another avatar were handed around during Valentine's Day, along with perfume and embarrassment and gossip and more romance. Mood swings and conversation shifts and grand promises and tiny lies. Leather and lace and flowers and swords decorated this Harlequin Romance world, this world of social exchange.

A day in Second Life lasts for four hours. These thin, short days flickered by like a movie, whirring and chattering with the events in this faraway place that had colonized my skull. The sun spun around me as I went through 24-hour cycles in the real world that were punctuated only by biobreaks. Sometimes I completely lost track of what time it was, as the Second Life days dictated my rhythm more than the real days. I continued to dive deep, Carmen was always a few levels deeper, and as we swam it became darker and colder and stranger.

Eventually, my health deteriorating, I was confronted with a decision: Which world did I prefer?

It's a potentially dangerous decision, and many arguments warn against, shall we say, *going native.* Avatars present a danger of isolation from not only the real world, but from ourselves. If an avatar is used too much, it can remove us from our real-world society. We lose touch with reality. The Stanford Institute for the Quantitative Study

of Society points out that with only five hours per week of Internet use, 15 percent of people interviewed reported a decrease in real-life social activities. They spent, for example, 25 percent less time talking on the phone to friends and family. Many American adults spend more time than that—an average of more than seven hours a week—playing games, and kids twice that much. This seems like a good reason to start looking more closely at what is going on.

Most of us have had the experience of trying to talk to someone while they're more engaged with their avatar, or zippered down into their fantasy world or game and reluctant to come out. Kids yell, "Be right there, Mom!" as they furiously pump the console to get leveled up before unplugging. Adults mumble half-replies to their kids as they coordinate their guild for the next raid. Roommates refuse to answer the phone. Friends don't IM back as quickly as they used to. People simply get lost in their avatar.

When we make an avatar, we invent a personality. In some cases, it may be the same personality, or a similar one, that we spend most of our days being. But often the alternative personality—the personality of the avatar—can become quite powerful. Part of the danger lies in how we control our avatar and how our avatar controls us. As people become more involved in the roles and rules of their avatar, they can also lose control of their alternative personality they have invented for that system. The alternative personality can become predominant and begin to take over the primary, daily one. This is the situation that most concerns parents. When they see their kid playing hours upon hours of World of Warcraft or Second Life or Lineage or Webkinz, they become concerned that their child will lose touch with the real-world society that is more important.

People sometimes prefer their avatar personas to their 'real' ones.

Your role as an avatar can take control of your life as a person. This was true long before online games and avatars. The classic example is the corporate executive who comes home and treats his children like employees. Or the marine who comes home and treats his family like recruits. The role has overcome the person and the context in which a person moves.

Losing control of one's life as a person, and therefore losing control of an alter-ego, can endanger others. One day in 2006, several Second Life avatars were having a roll in the virtual hay. A pretty normal day in Second Life—but when it was noticed that a few of them had been designed to look like prepubescents, many an eyebrow was raised. Avatars pretending to have sex with kids? Was this pedophilia? It wasn't clear. After all, an avatar that looks like an old woman may be driven by a young boy, and vice versa. The Second Life Teen Grid had been opened up for those under eighteen, so it was assumed the coast was clear enough and adult play could be allowed in the adult grid.

Emily Semaphore, one of the owners of Jailbait, an age-play region in Second Life, was quoted by the *Second Life Herald* as saying, "Being able to 'play' a kid in a 'safe' environment can be very healing for many people." Child-pornography prosecutors in the Netherlands disagreed and brought the case to court. It was later dropped because "the children avatars were not 'realistic enough.'" But this debate, as well as pressure from groups such as Familles de France, eventually contributed to Linden Lab hiring a company named Integrity-Aristotle to oversee identity verification in Second Life. Linden Lab made it clear that it would do nothing with the personal data, but Integrity-Aristotle

made no such claim. The end result was the beginning of a kind of driver's license. Avatars needed authentic identities that could be traced to a real human. People were furious about this enforced identity tracking, as well as with the company chosen to do it. They wanted their avatar to remain separate from their real identity, or at least to be able to decide themselves whether to be officially connected to them. Some users left. And although this "driver's license" reduced the ability to keep a psychological division and allowed for prosecution of the rampant alter-ego's owner, it could really do nothing to address the situation's cause. After all, what could Linden Lab do? Ban child avatars from the adult grid? What, then, would happen to the Harry Potter Fan Club?

Other anti-avatar arguments include the anti-social ones, which claim that spending social time online is less valuable and valid than spending time with people in the real world. People, and kids in particular, become shut-ins, pale, maggoty versions of their former selves. By spending too much time online they avoid spending time with anyone different from themselves. They start to lose their ability to interpret signs such as body language and intonation—important social signals that allow navigation through real, human society. They start to smell, and their hair becomes messy. They turn geeky and lose any social skills they may have had.

There are the arguments that claim video games are violent media that lead to violent behavior, and that exposure to violent media creates violent people. Parents cry danger, teachers see distraction, ministers warn of devil worship, and politicians makes speeches about corruption of the young. There's not much new about this argument. Parents, politicians, and pedagogues have always been afraid for our safety, and they have always made the same objections about each medium.

83

"The free access which many young people have to romances, novels, and plays has poisoned the mind and corrupted the morals of many a promising youth; and prevented others from improving the minds in useful knowledge. Parents take care to feed their children with wholesome diet; and yet how unconcerned about the provision for the mind, whether they are furnished with salutary food, or with trash, chaff, or poison?"
—Reverend Enos Hitchcock, *Memoirs of the Bloomsgrove Family,* 1790

"The indecent foreign dance called the Waltz was introduced ... at the English Court on Friday last ... It is quite sufficient to cast one's eyes on the voluptuous intertwining of the limbs, and close compressure of the bodies ... to see that it is far indeed removed from the modest reserve which has hitherto been considered distinctive of English females. So long as this obscene display was confined to prostitutes and adulteresses, we did not think it deserving of notice; but now that it is ... forced on the respectable classes of society by the evil example of their superiors, we feel it a duty to warn every parent against exposing his daughter to so fatal a contagion."
—The *Times* of London, 1816

"This new form of entertainment has gone far to blast maidenhood ... Depraved adults with candies and pennies beguile children with the inevitable result. The Society has prosecuted many for leading girls astray through these picture shows, but GOD alone knows how many are leading dissolute lives begun at the 'moving pictures.'"
—The Annual Report of the New York Society for the Prevention of Cruelty to Children, 1909

"Does the telephone make men more active or more lazy? Does [it] break up home life and the old practice of visiting friends?"
—Survey conducted by the Knights of Columbus Adult Education Committee, San Francisco Bay Area, 1926

"Delinquencies formerly restricted to adults are increasingly committed by young people and children ... All child drug addicts, and all children drawn into the narcotics traffic as messengers, with whom we have had contact, were inveterate comic-book readers. This kind of thing is not good mental nourishment for children!"
—Fredric Wertham, *Seduction of the Innocent,* 1954

"The effect of rock and roll on young people, is to turn them into devil worshippers; to stimulate self-expression through sex; to provoke lawlessness; impair nervous stability and destroy the sanctity of marriage. It is an evil influence on the youth of our country."
—Minister Albert Carter, 1956

"The disturbing material in Grand Theft Auto and other games like it is stealing the innocence of our children and it's making the difficult job of being a parent even harder ... I believe that the ability of our children to access pornographic and outrageously violent material on video games rated for adults is spiraling out of control."
—U.S. Senator Hillary Rodham Clinton, 2005

"In traveling through Second Life one quickly perceives that 'reality' in this universe is quite different. Actual photos and videos of pornography are pasted around certain regions. Users have the option to mimic sexual intercourse, themselves becoming scenes of rape, of bondage, bestiality, and scatophilia. ... [This is] a simple question of ethics, but, having given to minors the unrestricted ability to access these sites, the question becomes more important."
—French Conservative Organization, Familles de France, 2007

What horror!

Some find avatars to be gateways into a kind of hell. The avatar user becomes a schizophrenic personality, a hyper-violent, hyper-sexual, child-molesting psychopath, an outsider squinting out at the world, trapped inside an unhealthy body, abusing others, ultimately alone and unable to determine what is important.

Would I become this person if I continued to spend the majority of my waking hours in a geeky little fictional world inhabited by dressed-up strangers driving around in weird doll-machines? Would I continue to let my own life fall to the side and slide away? These are not uncommon questions. Millions have to make the same decisions every day.

I considered these questions thoroughly, slipped on my mask, and dove back in.

But why?

The more than 50 million people who choose to spend time as their avatars in virtual worlds probably think about such questions, or at least some of them do. Which gives us many millions of different answers.

For me, it's what I do. I travel, I paint, and I write. So I went back because flying around in a visual world of symbols and social interaction is where I live, what I live to build, and where I love to live. For me it was just a sensible decision. After all, I prefer to live the way I want as much as I can. Where I can fly. Where there is no such thing as scarcity or tragedy. Where I can stretch out my hand and create carpets, trees, castles, and mountains. Where—most of all—I can easily make smiles on the screen-lit faces of my far-flung friends as we dwell, laughing together, in the same dream. That is beautiful. That is a blending of the things in my life that I love most. I'm lucky I can experience this kind of travel.

Different people, of course, have different motivations, and patterns have been noted. Richard Bartle is an internationally recognized authority on virtual worlds, a pioneer of the MMORPG industry, and co-creator of the first text-based virtual world, MUD, back in 1979. He divides user motivations into four primary categories: the Explorers, the Socializers, the Achievers, and the Controllers. Explorers like to uncover beauty and show it to others. Socializers like to form groups, build social infrastructure, and throw parties. Achievers enhance the abilities of their avatars, increasing their power, wealth, and reputation, gaining social respect while doing it. Controllers are there to dominate, compete, and defeat. But whatever people use their avatars for, the avatars allow them to become more like what they want to be.

For some users, virtual worlds provide an alternative, online social life and actually provide access to more social living in real life. In August 2007, in the U.S. journal *CyberPsychology and Behavior*, researchers at Nottingham Trent University published a study called, "Social Interactions in Massively Multiplayer Online Role-Playing Gamers." Of the 1,000 gamers they interviewed, three quarters had made good friends online, half had met in real-life situations, a third had found themselves attracted to another gamer, and a tenth of them had developed physical relationships. So, it's not just that spending time as your avatar allows you to make new friends online; it opens the door for more social interaction in the real world.

Some would argue that sports are challenging and social and that playing them allows you to be competent and self-confident. When I was growing up, playing a lot of video games, adults often told me I should go out and play more sports. American football was the popular recommendation. But which, really, is more violent? Shooting pixels on a screen or breaking real bones on a football field from some kid jumping on your back because his dad's screaming from the bleachers?

85

Which really allows for increased social interaction? Which initiates group problem-solving and collaborative thinking?

Many spend time as their avatar not because they are addicted to a new thrill but because they are satisfying an old need. World of Warcraft, Second Life, and other role-playing games are engaging because they serve the primary human drives of socializing and being competent at a skill set. This has been confirmed by several researchers over the years. In 2006, the University of Rochester (N.Y.) and researchers at Immersyve Inc. interviewed 1,000 gamers in various MMOs. According to Richard Ryan, a motivational psychologist at the University, "…the psychological 'pull' of games is largely due to their capacity to engender feelings of autonomy, competence, and relatedness."

When someone slips into an avatar, they slip into the ability to be competent, to be who they want, and to spend time with a community that they choose. Being able to do all three things at once is a rare experience for many people—perhaps because of appearance, gender, race, sexuality, age, or simply the fact that they want more friends of different sorts, or more enemies, or for any of a million different reasons and justifications. For example, one wheelchair-bound 19-year-old man says, "I really love gaming. I love gaming because I can't really do what other people do because of my own problems as you see. But in games, I am just like everybody else, it's like I live my life there, and I'm not different, and I like that."

Everyone experiences some discomfort among their fellow humans; everyone has some way in which they would like a fantasy, or an improvement, or even just a break. Everyone is, on some level, fighting a great battle, and everyone finds life a bit difficult at times.

Avatars can give us an alternative, a break from daily hardships, and a space to practice for another try.

The first avatars and indeed the first large-scale virtual environment built for multi-user operation was were built for this very reason. Chip Morningstar and F. Randall Farmer developed Lucasfilm's Habitat specifically so that hospitalized children could have an alternative, and a break from a limbo life in a hospital bed. The system, built on Commodore 64s, gave the kids a chance to go on quests together when they couldn't even get out of a hospital bed. Morningstar adopted the term "avatar" from Hindu mythology to describe the graphical representation of a user. This happened in California, in 1985.

The avatar is a Californian invention that uses computer software. It is a technological, automated American Dream. This is important for understanding why people use avatars.

The "American Dream" tells us that we can become who we want, and we can profit by doing so. It is the dream of independence and success and that core ability to make yourself into who and what you want. During the population explosion of Los Angeles, in 1931, James Adams published a book titled *The Epic of America* and in it he describes The American Dream as, "that dream of a land in which life should be better and richer and fuller for every man, with opportunity for each according to his ability or achievement." This dream of profit and social mobility via industry wasn't, nor is it now, particularly *American*. The immigrants to L.A. were pre-industrial nomads, rootless and willing to give up their homes, friends, and families back East or in Europe in exchange for a promise of a world they could build themselves. It was a "My land, my imagination" mentality. These were people who didn't fit within a community of strict rules, who didn't recognize themselves as members of that community and because they were nomadic they were also community builders. So they built a new kind of community that allowed them to be freer, and more recognized as individuals with less social pressure. They packed their bags, walked away from their past, and started on an ambitious and strange project that we now call Los Angeles.

The same thing has happened in Second Life. These two sets of immigrants were not only demographically similar, as I've pointed out, but they were also moved by many of the same motivations as immigrants to Second Life and other virtual worlds. In 2007, I surveyed, either via form or interview, more than 300 virtual-world residents. Some interviews were with the ten percent who had been spending about as much time in-world as a full-time job. What I found made a kind of grim sense: These people had assembled their own synthetic communities because they had none on hand in the real world. Most of them came from small families, had no siblings, came from small communities, traveled a great deal. Eighty percent of these users lived in cities more than 100 miles from where they were born. More than a third moved to a new city every four years. About a third were Asian, a little over half were male, and all had a desire to leave a system they disliked. Avatars had allowed them to create their own community.

Avatars also give these same people an opportunity to explore a place that is safer than what the modern world seems to afford. If I believe the media I notice around me, the world seems to be getting a lot more dangerous. Compared to a decade ago the danger level in the United States is probably not higher, but the fear level certainly is. Parents are less inclined to let their children play alone in the streets. Governments are less inclined to advise their citizens to travel abroad. Gangs roam in front of your home, terrorists lurk in your neighborhood alley, danger supposedly hides under every bridge. Living in Los Angeles, I hear an awful lot of noise about how dangerous it is outside. Newspapers, radios, televisions, and airport ceiling-robots scream about the dangers nearby. We are pushed by our media to risk less. We are told by our police force to avoid strangers. We are told to be afraid. We are told to stay at home. And so we go into the virtual world.

Avatars offer an alternative to the "American Dream" of decentralized cities full of anonymous faces, depersonalized living, mass media, and fear.

Avatars, self-assembled constellations of the individual and the community, allow a way to return to something that is central to the human experience. They bring us back to a smaller society of people whom we know and care about and trust.

Ironically, avatars offer a return to pre-industrial, pre-automated societies; to small groups of families and friends that once existed only in villages.

As my friend, the novelist William Kowalski, writes: "Is this an attempt for us to get back to the life that really matters—the symbolic life? Is this our weird American version of waking up and saying that the world we actually live in, the world we've created for ourselves—strip malls, pollution, racism, meaningless jobs—is absolute bullshit, and not worth living?"

Carmen's take on it is similar: "One of the things that fuels synthetic worlds is that the society we live in is so rigid and the roles are so over-determined, yet none of them works. People are rebuilding western society inside these worlds, just as they did in the Renaissance."

Simply put, avatars fill in the social blanks of contemporary society and in doing so, if used too much, offer real dangers.

People get more and more deeply involved, passing more and more heartbeats, exploring broader landscapes with their avatars, playing these "games" and letting what may be an unsatisfying or potentially unconnected lives—their first lives—fade and fall to the side in favor of something that often feels like a cross between a movie and a dream, perhaps because their real lives are a nightmares. It only makes sense that another life offering greater engagement might start to compete with one that, for many people, is not what they'd hoped. They have another option.

Virtual worlds are the American Dream, second edition—a response to the American Dream, first edition.

Sticks and Stones May Break My Bones but Karate Is Not Sexy

"One thing we found out is that women don't want to be spaceships. I've shown Eve Online videos to lots of girls, and their eyes just glaze over... but I show it to guys and they're like, 'Hell yeah!' Our research into this, by hiring more girls into CCP and asking them what they want to do, shows that they want to be people. They don't want to be spaceships."
—Crowd Control Productions (CCP) CEO Hilmar Petursson.

One day I found out rather dramatically that an online action can have a real physical reaction. I was clowning around with the crowd on Enigma Island. Rraven and Dezire were having a yard sale. There were some spaceship parts, a few random pieces of clothes, shoes, paintings that Dez had made, some parachutes, jewelry, and the occasional set of wings. Travis Maeterlinck, dressed in his usual kit—fox head and enough weapons to make Rambo run—had teleported in from his Fur Kingdom for a visit, probably looking for guns. We were all a bit bored. Fortunately, at least for me, I'd found some great karate animations and so I got to practicing my moves. It was classic Bruce Lee stuff: roundhouse back kick, forward punch, ground sweep, inward chop. Having spent years doing real-life karate, this seemed so far beyond absurd that I couldn't stop myself from laughing while my skinny boneman of an avatar pretended to be tough. I assumed it was a joke for others as well. I'm not the type who shows off like this in real life. For me, this was simple avatar fun.

While I threw punches, the usual crowd of shoppers came through to look at the sale..

Then *she* walked in.

She was dressed in leopard-skin leotards and smoked her cigarette through a foot-long cigarette holder. Orange eyes, long black fingernails, and a gait that would slay a lion.

I was in love. Again.

Every red-blooded male knows that flexing your muscles gets the babes, so I threw a lethal display of a forward chop followed by a tight back roundhouse. As I went into the second set, I was confident as a rap star. My deadly mettle would leave her wooed and shaky-kneed. She would be mine.

Hyah!, I typed.

She continued to shop and I continued to assume it was a woman.

Undeterred, I threw a few more moves and added a little commentary along the lines of, "Pighed Stonecutter shoots a sharp sidekick to impress any potential onlookers dressed in cat outfits."

Still no reaction.

After a good minute or two of this Dezire kindly said in my direction, "Sometimes, Pighed, the direct approach is the best."

Stopping my karate kicks, I popped in a cigarette, walked up to the avatar in the leopard-skin, faced her directly, and said, "Wanna fuck!?" My avatar stood there, shirtless, a stupid cigarette sending up a little line of digital smoke I had paid a good five cents for. Truth be told, I was a virgin in SL, so I had no idea what she would do.

She didn't move or even say anything for at least two seconds, and I began to wonder if she'd heard me. I thought I'd get a clever quip out of her, or some kind of silly slam, a flirtation, perhaps, or at least a witty rejection. But after this moment of silence her avatar leapt forward and ran into mine, her head hitting me in the chin. My avatar bounced back a good meter and then did a little animation to show that he'd regained his balance. A tinny MIDI version of "Mreeeoow! Hiss!" crackled out of my speakers, and I realized it was from the cat-woman who'd just run into me.

I was so shocked that I forgot all my slick, in-world karate moves, and in the real world the attack caused me to gasp and pull back from the monitor. I took my hands away from the keyboard and realized that my avatar had become, somehow, my body.

Avatars have bodies. They can be touched or wounded, and they have hygiene. This happens for many reasons, but four of the primary reasons are because of how our brains are wired, how we use our avatars, how we build them, and how we take care of them.

As for how we are physically wired, between your ears, in the inferior parietal cortex, there's a microscopic cluster of gunk called mirror neurons. Mirror neurons serve a very important function; they allow you to identify with another person's actions, specifically when it relates to a goal-oriented action. In essence, when you watch someone do something that is familiar, you relate to their actions as if they were your own. Your neurons are literally firing as if you were doing the action yourself. If you have ever watched an athlete move and felt your body twitch as if you were doing the act, or if you have ever watched someone get hit on the head and flinched yourself—that's your mirror neurons at work. Mirror neurons, technically, are neurons that fire both when you do the action and when you see someone else do it.

"The main functional characteristic of mirror neurons is that they become active both when the monkey makes a particular action (for example, when grasping an object or holding it) and when it observes another individual making a similar action."
—Giacomo Rizzolatti, Luciano Fadiga, Leonardo Fogassi and Vittorio Gallese, the discoverers of mirror neurons

It is the actions and appearances of avatars that allow us to identify with them and gets the mirror neurons hot. They may be just pixels, but your brain responds as if they were human. Our wiring quickly bridges the gap between the real and the fictional.

The second reason an avatar has a body is because we, as users, are active. Okay, we're sitting on our asses, but we're actively engaged in making decisions and solving problems. We are always doing something with our avatars: driving them, working through them, finding new ones, manipulating objects, achieving goals, learning, changing, and interacting with the surroundings and other avatars nearby. As opposed to the case of television or movies, in which we passively sit and watch the narrative happen to a character with whom we may or may not identify, with avatars we are asked to act out the story, move around in it, and affect it. This engages our mirror neurons even more so, but it also means that we develop a more intimate and linked relationship with the avatar. I tell my avatar to jump, and when he does I feel closer to him than if he did not.

The third reason an avatar has a body is because of how we build them. I asked 130 people whether their avatars were like themselves in height, weight, and charisma. Seventy percent across the board said yes, for each element. This filtering of the factual into fictional is a widespread habit. Criminals, for example, living under false identity generally use data that has some relation to their real lives (a Mark picking the name Matt or Mike as a pseudonym, for example, and inventing a fake phone number and address that has many of the same numbers—try it, you'll probably find you do the same). We generally build a second version of ourselves that has some bearing on who we are in the real world. When you make an avatar of the same gender, age, and race, it feels like you on a psycho-physiological level. You can identify with it. There are very few morbidly obese, elderly, or handicapped avatars in virtual worlds, but many who are so in the real world still make avatars who are like them in some way. Around seventy percent of people who build avatars like themselves also feel pretty good about themselves. Most of us like who we really are in real life.

We groom our avatars. When you spend time with your avatar you begin to have a sense of both private and public hygiene. By private hygiene, I mean things done out of personal interest involving convenience, efficiency, and the ability to communicate, such as sorting, managing, and categorizing possessions. You have to make sure you know where things are, keep them organized and clear, maintain keyboard shortcuts and macros for particular functions, and properly install recent upgrades—looking after your avatar's functionality. Public hygiene has to do with giving others a sense of how to interact with you. This includes portraying and constantly clarifying the archetype, role, or class, of the character, and it includes conveying a sense of pride in the community. Changing clothes from time to time, making sure that they reflect the social role or the game rules, and keeping the avatar well built, in terms of shape, texture maps, and animations. As with real-world hygiene, not everyone is sensitive to the same issues, but everyone lives with the consequential judgment of others. Psychologically, this is how avatars work.

Dutchy Flammand, Second Life

CAR IS AVATAR IS PROSTHETI

"The car has become the carapace, the protective and aggressive shell, of urban and suburban man."
—Marshall McLuhan

McLuhan, a top Canadian media theorist, pointed out that the car "extended" the human foot as a prosthesis. McLuhan's point was that our technology, as we use it, fundamentally changes us. Avatars are, like cars, another example of a prosthetic technology that is changing us.

Cars and avatars are quite similar: Cars and avatars are both interactive, they represent us socially and culturally, they transport us, they're an expression of personality, they allow us to get things done, we travel in them, we talk in them, and you can buy useful and/or decorative accessories for them that often cost more than the car or avatar itself.

These accessories come as both utility and decoration. Tool-based accessories are needed for performance and for following the rules of the road, while decorative accessories are there for social bolstering and establishing archetypes and rituals. Painting flames on the side of the car sends a different message than having a little silver jaguar on the hood. Note that we associate our car with ourselves. In fact, more than that, we don't even differentiate. For example, we say, "He ran the red light and hit me," not, "He ran the red light and hit my car." The vehicle is an extension of our

body. Already there's an emerging industry in sales and advertisements for avatars, and this trend will probably continue as the years roll by. Cars and avatars are vehicles that fit your lifestyle. And the more we use them the more we need them.

Avatars are a psychological prosthetic. It's an anomaly far more curious than a peg leg, glass eye, or hook hand because the use of an avatar isn't immediately necessary. It appears to be for a game. But it is more useful than something that would help us grasp or pinch, such as a bionic arm, or a pair of pliers, or a well-worn leather glove, because an avatar allows us access to a much wider variety of items with a much more intricate level of control.

Avatars teleport our psyche. It is more capable of bridging distances than shoes, or planes, or cars because it puts us immediately next to another person, much like a phone does. It's a much more efficient vehicle than a car or a plane because it can transport us further, faster, and more immediately. Unlike the prosthetics of the ear-replacing telephone or the eye-replacing television, it is a prosthetic that replaces the entire body.

Three cars, three people

An avatar is also a prosthetic with prosthetics. Accessories, such as information management tools, weapons, and enhancements that allow for a game-based avatar to level up or accessories of social engagement such as the meter-long penises of the Furries, are all attached to your attachment. The clothes and word balloons and animations and messages are all prosthetics of your prosthetic. And perhaps the very environments that avatars move in—the mountains or dungeons or backgrounds that frame them—are their prosthetics. As we've noted, the real-estate of a virtual world is there simply to frame the avatar.

*When you enter the machine
the machine enters you.*

Prosthetics, and the different versions of bodily reality have been brewing for some time. Around the turn of the millennium all five of the senses became mediated. By the year 2000 humanity began to convert sensoral experience into databases. Hearing was mediated first, with telephony in the late 1800s, and the concept of television was hot on its heels, just a few years later, with people like Alexander Graham Bell proposing a "Photophone" and a Russian by the name of Constantin Perskyi using the term *television* at the 1900 World's Fair in Paris. Though Nikola Tesla filed a patent in the U.S. in 1898 for work with *teleoperation* (U.S. Patent No. 613,809), it wasn't until about 70 years later that *telerobotics* began to mediate touch. In 1994 I experienced, for the first time, mediated smell and taste: A printer-like device puffed out various aromatic "inks" that combined to give my nose and tongue a taste of the Internet. It smelled like roses. All of these sense-mediation technologies now live in digital formats, so we've evidently succeeded in packing the senses into the machine, shipping it across the Internet, and unpacking it on the other end.

Nobody knows exactly how many avatars there are. Frankly, I don't care, since by the time you're done reading this sentence the number will have changed. But conservatively we can say that there are about 200 million people using avatars and about 10 percent of them spend more than 10 hours a day doing this.

There will always be more avatars than people driving them, and people are constantly creating new accounts, so we can rest assured that, at best, our numbers will be both inaccurate and obsolete. But that aside, I suspect that there are over half a billion avatars and over two hundred million people driving them. According to MMOGData (mmogdata.voig.com), which follows 122 different virtual worlds, the absolute number of contributions is approximately 35 million. But avatars aren't just 3-D. Let's just guesstimate users from the big virtual worlds, for starters; World of Warcraft (9m), RuneScape (5m), Guild Wars (3m), plus approximately the approximately hundred other virtual worlds, summing up to well over 30 million players. We can add in some of the other immersive worlds that are not exclusively 3-D, such as NeoPets (70m), Habbo Hotel (54m), Gaia (10m), MapleStory (50m), and Cyworld (20m). If we throw in things like Facebook (30m) and others, the number of avatars gets large fast. Around half a billion. But some of those players' accounts from different systems will be the same person, so let's divide it in half. These numbers are always problematic since, for example, it's commonly understood that Second Life has 10 million avatar accounts, but people could set up as many accounts as they wanted.

Confidently, I can say that there are at least two hundred million people using avatars of some sort. And we've also shown that ten percent of these are hard-core users, people that spend more than nine hours a day as their avatar.

93

Pixeleen Mistral, Second Life

Over twenty million people spend more than nine hours per day as their avatar.

These hard-core users have gone native. They have crossed an important line. I've experienced this myself. It causes emotional, physical, social, intellectual, and perhaps spiritual shifts. Not only would I walk around seeing things in the world that reminded me of Second Life, I caught myself thinking at times that I could affect objects in the same way that I was able to affect objects as my avatar. I had the feeling that there was some "Undo" function, a <ctrl-z> function, or that I could create geometry out of thin air. When I was away from the machine, I felt as though I had undergone a kind of terminal amputation. With this ability to dislocate functions of my body, with the mediation of my senses, and with this new prosthetic that allowed me to move to another place, I had stepped across a mysterious and fateful line.

Me and some twenty million other people.

Perhaps some 50 years from now we will look back and note that this was the period when our bodies became obsolete, replaced by the more flexible, interesting, transportable, replaceable, and controllable prosthetic of avatars. Perhaps the transition will be gradual but clearly seen in retrospect, much as cars replaced horses. After all, the car was more flexible, interesting, transportable, replaceable, and controllable than was the horse. And so the horse was replaced with the prosthetic of the car.

Or perhaps now, at this moment when avatars have allowed us to visit friends, make new family, work for our daily bread, drink our daily wine on virtual cliffs, perhaps now, when our core emotional and social needs can be displaced into virtual environments and when even the people that are next to us in a virtual world may or may not be real humans but scripted autonomous avatars and chatbot characters—perhaps now is when technology no longer becomes an extension of us, but we become an extension of it. Whether it is half avatar or half human, we are being propelled into a new world where the body is built as much as it is born, where it is tool as much as decoration, and where even its existence is a question.

The avatar is the usher of a post-human era.

This is not science fiction, but "progress." This is simply the face of humanity as we strap on more and more tools, embedding them into our bodies, growing into them, improving limbs and replacing organs, allowing them to change into us as we change into them. It's how we grow into our imaginations, and how our dreams becomes real.

"WHERE THERE IS ID THERE WILL BE EGO."

But I have a hard time with this idea. It's not that I have a hard time accepting that I use prosthetics, or that some of my life has been spent in non-physical worlds, or even that these little cartoon characters of ourselves might be the harbingers of a new kind of evolution. What keeps me awake at night is the question of who "I" am when I drive an avatar. The core problem an avatar presents is, what is self? Books such as Sherry Turkle's *Life on the Screen* and Donna Haraway's *Simians, Cyborgs, and Women* explore online identity. But I haven't seen many books that address the question of a person who runs his own club of alts, or one who builds two avatars, one the master and one the slave. How far out does an identity extend? What are its limits? Why do I think my avatar is me? If my avatar had an avatar would that also be me?

The psychology of avatars extends into the real world just as our personalities extend into the virtual. Avatars encourage a fracturing of psyche and personality. Almost like cable cutters, they split us open and strip our different personas into individual threads, so we can splice them with other threads on the other end—other people who are doing the same thing. When I consider that my multiple personal identities and my various social footprints are all embodied in my avatars, it almost sounds like a kind of Multiple Personality Order. Maybe avatars comb out the sometimes tangled parts of our personalities and allow us to view them in the light to assess their health, value, and identities. What fragment of my personality does that avatar best represent? Why did I choose it? What would two of my avatars discuss if, somehow, they could talk to one another?

You are the trunk of the identity tree, and your avatars are the leaves.

I have worked with Dr. Yanon Volcani for years on various interactive narrative and character systems. Dr. Volcani has more than 30 years of experience in the field of psychology (specifically with clinical assessment, research, and treatment). He is now a specialist in content analysis for autonomous systems.

Dr. Volcani once told me that the avatar is built separate from us so that we may view ourselves. Externalizing an aspect of our personality allows us to control that aspect rather than be controlled by it (although as I have mentioned, occasionally we can lose control) and nurture and develop it as external to us. The externalized aspect of one's personality is often a pure archetype, our "inner hero." We use this inner hero just as a child uses a doll. Avatars allow us to play and experiment with new worlds, with new versions of ourselves, and by doing that we rehearse for real life.

"Our avatar," Yanon said, "is us in transformation. Being able to watch ourselves creates a reflective state that's good for us. We reflect on ourselves as the compassionate observer. We're both engaged and observing at the same time. It's basic play therapy. We are in it, but not. We know it's not really real. But it is a close approximation—close enough to engage us. Freud called this Cathect. Physically speaking, avatars engage our dopamine system. The extreme side of dopamine is the creation of addiction to terrible things like heroin. But dopamine is like honey; it sticks us to things. If we watch the endocrine system, we see games really having an impact. Games need to move from dopamine into oxytosin and vasopressin. If we want to look at games endocrinologically, that is...."

"So, it's possible that a part of myself can control myself?" I asked him.

"That's the whole fundamental, most basic notion, in psychology. The core question of psychology is: 'Why do we do what we do?' Or, 'Why don't we do what we should do?' 'Why do smart people do stupid things?' Because we are not in control of certain aspects of ourselves that dominate our behavior. Avatars are a way to manage and develop and relate to the totality of aspects of ourselves and our unconscious. We have multiple selves that are cohesive, or coherent with each other. That's hard to maintain! Very limited versions of self are tolerated. There are a lot of aspects of self, but they're often in conflict with each other, and that causes distress. That's the Freudian point of the unconscious, Freud's example of wanting to choke your mother, the tip of the iceberg being our conscious mind. Here's an important distinction between Jung and Freud: Freud considered left brain and right brain and said, 'Where there is Id there will be Ego.' But Jung said that you have to relate to and expand symbols of personality that we find and build, otherwise you are only making the symbol a sign. Otherwise you can lose control of it."

I told Yanon a story about losing control of an avatar. I'm assured by an anonymous but reliable party that, despite sitting at the edges of believability, the following or something like it actually happened.

Once upon a time there were a man and a woman who spent a lot of time with their avatars together in Second Life, grooming and growing their role-play fiction into a complex citadel of imagination. It became their private world. Eventually they called each other on the phone and then, after some time, they met in the real world. They continued to dress up in differ- ent costumes and play different games together in Second Life, often changing

the rules of their games and their roles. One day—in real life—the man put on some diapers and called himself a baby, and the woman put on some boots and called herself a mistress, and the two of them went to a nearby shopping mall in a Midwestern American town. The woman had a short whip with her, and the man had laxative pills. Before going into the mall the man ate the laxatives and, after about a half hour in the mall, had to use the bathroom. But the rules of their game did not allow him to use the bathroom. The rules of the game only allowed him to use his diapers. The rules of the game also said that the woman had to discipline him, and had to use her riding crop to do so.

Yanon whispered, "Oh, Jesus.…"

I had to laugh a bit. But I like the story because these people found a profound freedom and I admire them for that. The story also makes me feel like I'm not too weird. Yet.

Yanon regained his composure and said, "It's easy to get attached to avatars and the ways of being that are outside the scope of everyday life. An avatar affords us that. Look, let's face it; avatars are fulfilling. So we want to make our first life more like our second life. Kids do that really well—they play Superman and then actually *feel* like Superman. Most of us have done this. For example, when I was eight, my best buddy and I used to protect the public from crime with our x-ray vision. We knew we were playing, but we pushed it to the edge because we really wanted it to be true. If we feel too constricted in daily life (and we really all do to some extent), we don't get to do these kinds of things. As we continue to spend time in these places, we get to act out in ways we never really have before, and it's so seductive that we want to bring it out into the real world."

A company named Fabjectory develops real-world copies of World of Warcraft, Nintendo Mii, and Second Life avatars. For about US$75, you can order a small foam or plastic doll of your avatar. It's a different way of getting your avatar into the real world. Diapers are not included.

Renaissance Faire goers

KAJIRA, RADDICK, AND INVOLUNTARY SPEED DATING SERVICES

There is virtual and real, fiction and fact, the person and their alter-ego, the individual and their community, and all of these things start to lose definition when you pack them into this container of identity called the avatar, and each of these elements seems to feed and increase the power of the others. It's a circulatory system of identity. In my travels, this came to a head when I continued to learn about master-slave relationships.

Master-slave interaction in Second Life is mildly popular. Of the 1,000 or so avatars that I met in Second Life, I would guess around 200 actively participated in slave-master play. That matches up with some statistics released by New World Notes in September 2007, which indicated that 4 of the 20 most popular areas in Second Life offer BDSM (bondage, domination, sadism, masochism) role play. For the record, I found it all to be a bit loathsome. When I built for Goreans (or on occasion, Furries), it was always a little strange to be putting up a floating buttress and hear someone say, "Girl goes to get Master a cool drink of water." Though I was usually well treated and occasionally well paid, I never cared much for the BDSM scene.

Gorean and Furry master-slave relations were partially what caused Familles de France to publish on its website a scathing public rebuke of Linden Lab's product, eventually resulting in Linden Lab's requirement of verifiable personal information on each user. This sent ripples through the Second Life community, as many residents had been edging into more and more extreme forms of role play, until Second Life had begun to acquire a reputation as a system of perverts and porn dogs.

In an effort to entertain myself, understand Gor, and get a better handle on these odd interactions, I interviewed an avatar named Raddick Szymborska. Raddick is about a year old. He calls himself a "matchmaker of sorts" who provides "involuntary speed-dating services."

Other people call these slave auctions.

Raddick told me that there is no shortage of people wanting to be slaves in one manner or another; he advertises that he's looking, and they come apply. The interactions at the auctions allow people to explore different sides of themselves, be it dominant or submissive. First, the slave is stripped and put in a public cage, available for interested buyers to come examine the merchandise. Buyers look over the slaves as if they were examining horses. The slaves are taken below ground, and then the bidding begins. Each is called in turn, and Raddick holds back the "more valuable stock" until the end. This is interesting to me because, in the end, it's really an art competition. It's a self-portrait auction.

Raddick and Pighed talkin' on the sofas.

The slave is made to stand and "present" for the audience. As Raddick put it, "Some slaves are compliant, some, eager to be sold, some fight the collar. These are all opportunities to explore the role."

I asked him about the role of master.

Raddick Szymborska: In general, a Master or Mistress is the owner, caretaker, protector, and manager of the slave. It is a narrow framework for interaction. It is 'I am buying you, I have you now, here are my rules, lets see how you do.' In more general terms, the Master has complete control of the slave, and holds the life of the slave in his hands. The Master or Mistress must be strong, wise, and exhibit good judgment in the management of their slaves for the relationship to be satisfactory.

Pighed Stonecutter: can the slave leave?

Raddick Szymborska: In a permanent sale, no. The slave is the property of the buyer, like buying a hammer.

Pighed Stonecutter: but what does that mean? let's say that i buy someone and they decide that i'm a jackass and they want out. the slave can just quit the interaction, correct?

Raddick Szymborska: Well, yes, everything in SL is consensual, ultimately. However, if one doesn't want to break the roleplay, one is stuck, unless the Master releases the slave. The Master/Slave relationship, if practiced properly, is simply another expression of a meaningful human interaction. Being a Master and having a slave is more than 'hey baby, go get me a drink.'

Pighed Stonecutter: it's a support / nurture / guide role, right?

Raddick Szymborska: Yes, that is an excellent way to put it.

Twice during our discussion Raddick pointed out that he has never met any slave in real life. He has a strict rule against it. He knows of about ten other slave traders in Second Life, but has no idea if it is as important for them not to cross the line into the real world.

The phone rang. It was Carmen

"Piggie, I've got a problem. A real problem."

This wasn't a joke, and she wasn't playing a role.

"There are real-life slave traders after me. They're after several people right now. There are a dozen or so of them and they're collecting slaves in the Gorean marketplaces and then tracking them down in real life."

"How do you know this? How do you know it's not some bored junior high kid?"

"It's all too well constructed. Oh, shit. They're sending me messages on Yahoo now."

I suggested she leave the computer alone for a bit, said good night, and hung up the phone, thinking it all seemed a bit overblown. It was probably just some bored junior high kid.

A day or two later she confessed that she hadn't left her computer alone and that these "recruiters" had continued to pester her.

"Three things happened," she began. "First I started getting instant messages at 5 and 10 p.m.—always at this time and always from this group of people. It was only a little weird when sometimes four of them, from the same group, would IM me, as if they were coordinating, but it was when they started to ask me (at night), 'Why are you still awake? You should be in bed,' that I realized they were trying to cross a line. Now, this was in Yahoo, not in Second Life, so they had already crossed one line with me, and with this real-life stuff they were trying to cross another. They were trying to impose borders on when I go to sleep and control what I did with my time.

"But on top of that they were very insistent about who I see and when, and they seemed to be trying to close my social circle into a smaller and smaller ring. It was like they were trying to make themselves more important in my life. They were treating me as if I were emotionally isolated and unstable. I mean, if you're a 19-year-old isolated kid, and these people are giving you attention, telling you they love you, what would you do? You'd hang out with them. It is manipulation by guilt, isolation, and mock sensitivity."

They would ask Carmen to stay, express sadness when she'd want to leave, and ask her if someone had ordered her to be mean to them, the implication being that she was ordered about anyway. And they insisted on getting increasingly personal. Over the past few weeks her new friends had asked her questions about her personal life, where she lived, what she did, who she knew, where she grew up, and so on—more than was appropriate. She refused to answer these questions and concentrated on the game. The mysterious group became more and more persistent. She would mute one avatar, only to find a different one, later that day, asking her the same questions. Then someone on a completely different system would find her, sending her messages of a similar sort, always working to get more personal.

Carmen continued, "When they said, at one point, 'when you come to us' I realized, for sure, there was something wrong. Think of those words. They imply that at some point I will make an agreement to visit them in their terms and territory. This game is oriented around meeting on neutral ground. They're doing everything they can to change that. These are 'families' that obtain people, generally newbies, who are emotionally needy. It's one thing to take disco dancing into the system, or money out of it. That's an 'Oh, Wow' kind of technical feat, for a game to do that. But to say that people's lives are being captured is different. For most people, its not what they signed up for."

The virtual was becoming real for Carmen, too. Even if it had been a bored junior high kid, or a collection of them, that was badgering her, the impact was still quite real. During an email conversation the month before she had said, "Where I think people get banged up emotionally is that they do not really expect to encounter themselves involved in a practical experience of catharsis by crashing into more or less pure archetype. People are prepared for theater as theory. They are not really prepared to participate and be affected in their lives. People also do not think, when they go into a world, that they are bringing themselves with them, but they are. They bring their emotions, thoughts, spiritual beliefs, and sexuality. Through these things, particularly their sexuality, they bring their bodies into the world. My thing in virtual worlds has been personal power. I have ruled and been ruled. Of the two, the experience of being ruled is more valuable; it taught me more about my self. It forced me to confront history and baggage. For me, experiences in synthetic worlds have been a way of uncovering more layers of self; a discipline, if you will, not unlike that connected with learning an art form. I would not change anything."

Creepy as slavery role-play may be for some of us, it probably has to do with being able to see the externalized aspect of the self, as Yanon said. Carmen, after all, was a drama queen. She was a master at being a slave and often wrote articles for the Second Life Herald, going to great effort to point out what everyone suspected; playing around with slave-master games can be dangerous.

As the saying goes, just because you're paranoid doesn't mean they're not after you. Carmen's instant messages kept appearing, asking why she was still awake, and when she didn't respond or blocked the account, a different message would come from a different direction insisting she was being hurtful. So as most people do when threatened, Carmen put distance between herself and her aggressors. She cancelled her accounts, spent time with a different group. After a few months, the messages had all been blocked, the accounts had all been cancelled, and the mysterious tribe that was trying to seduce her gave up and evaporated into the mysts from which they'd come.

It was not too surprising that Carmen would end up being pursued by what appeared to be slave traders. After all, since 1993, she has always had the greatest alertness of anyone I have met for what the Internet can do and become, and why. The Humdog, sniffing around in the underground, has a good nose for finding truffles.

I met another person who was coming from, let's say, the other side. She was a real slave who was trying to find her way out of her reality with a fiction. It was part of a therapy that had been recommended, apparently, by someone who was her personal counselor.

When Ms. Doe (who asked me not to use any of her names) was 17, her boyfriend thought it would be a funny joke to "sell" her to several men he knew. They had been playing bondage games, and eventually this led to more and more extreme forms of "play." The transaction went down as planned. Out in the woods of western Michigan, Ms. Doe was put into a van and then driven to a small house in northern Minnesota, which began four years of slavery. This experience included rape, bondage, and having her arm publicly broken in front of the other slaves for simply touching a computer.

Eventually Ms. Doe was sold to a third owner. At 23, she fell ill, and her current master didn't have enough money to pay her hospital bill, so instead he gave her $100, dropped her off at a bus stop, and she was introduced to freedom. When she got home, her family didn't believe her story.

Since then she's spent time in Second Life working toward a healthy reconciliation with a past that she has, at times, trouble remembering. Through her in-world role-play of being a slave, she is trying to gain a perspective from which to view herself.

My own hunch is that the story she told me really happened. According to the U.S. Department of State's 2004 *Trafficking in Persons Report*, human trafficking is the third most profitable criminal activity in the world (led only by drug and arms trafficking). An estimated US$9.5 billion is annually generated from trafficking activities, with another $4 billion annually attributed to the worldwide brothel industry. Of the approximately 700,000 people trafficked across international borders each year, seventy percent are female.

Frankly, Mrs. Doe is a bit of a mess. I found talking with her rather empty. Either she's messed up because she's making all of this up, or she's messed up because it really happened. Either way, though, it seems that her avatar helps her untangle these realities and fictions and learn what's important in her real life.

[18:33] Mrs. Doe: it was an office i was instructed to clean...
[18:34] Mrs. Doe: was left as a trap... i knew i was not supposed to touch it
[18:34] Pighed Stonecutter: ... but you did anyway?
[18:35] Mrs. Doe: yes... was tempting... a chance i had to take... i never did again though.
[18:35] Pighed Stonecutter: so were you trying to email someone?
[18:36] Mrs. Doe: yes, that was my thought... but one keypress and it started beeping like crazy
[18:36] Pighed Stonecutter: what happened then?
[18:37] Mrs. Doe: they came for me
[18:39] Mrs. Doe: was taken to the hall... everyone was called... they announced what i did
[18:41] Mrs. Doe: and broke my wrist.
[18:41] Pighed Stonecutter: in front of the others? as a demonstration?
[18:41] Mrs. Doe: yes
[18:42] Pighed Stonecutter: how, if i may ask?
[18:43] Mrs. Doe: a rig they had... my arm strapped in... a weight that fell
[18:43] Pighed Stonecutter: and did they help you heal or were you left to limp like that?
[18:44] Mrs. Doe: yes... once i was done throwing up and finished cleaning the office, it was set in a cast.
[18:44] Pighed Stonecutter: by the same guy the broke it?
[18:44] Mrs. Doe: yes
[18:45] Pighed Stonecutter: and what did you have to say to him while he set the bone?
[18:45] Pighed Stonecutter: was there interaction?
[18:45] Mrs. Doe: i thanked him when he was done
[18:46] Pighed Stonecutter: did you thank him for setting it or breaking it?
[18:46] Mrs. Doe: setting it.

Montserrat Snakeankle
Second Life

Celebrities and Millions of Us

Molotov Alva is a star in an HBO series. He's been featured in *Time* magazine. He is represented by UTA, one of the top acting agencies in Los Angeles, he's been considered for an Oscar, and he's making more on his licensing deal than most actors are today. The series is about a guy who "uploads," or leaves his real world behind and chooses another in Second Life.

Molotov Alva, Second Life
(Photo: Douglas Gayeton)

But Molotov isn't a human. He's an avatar. Molotov is an *idoru* (Japanese for *idol*, which can also mean a celebrity who doesn't have a physical body). The television series was written and directed by Douglas Gayeton, a filmmaker, photographer, and designer. Douglas created not just the film Molotov stars in, but Molotov as well. We spoke about avatars one afternoon, and he pointed out that social networks are becoming "avatarized." The avatar might start in Second Life, but then that personality appears on the person's blog, becomes their email name, and then in the social networks the avatar name continues. He talked about "bifurcated personalities" that exhibit behavior specific to each of the platforms that their avatar is on, behavior that might or might not be anything like their real-world behavior.

As Douglas put it, "The value of the avatar is like Homer Simpson, or any character created by a comedian. That character lives and has a different identity from the actor. The Blues Brother, for example, is not Dan Akroyd."

Millions of people have seen Molotov's face. People identify with him. People think they know a little about him, about who he is, and where he came from. And like any celebrity, he has a certain way of dressing, of walking, of moving his head. He has his camera accessory and his way of talking that is different from Douglas.

The line between an avatar and a celebrity grows thinner by the day.

Douglas, meanwhile, works in the real world as the Chief Creative Officer for Millions of Us, a virtual-worlds boutique based in San Francisco. Millions of Us began as a Second Life service bureau and has expanded into a 31-person organization of engineers and artists building virtual products in multiple virtual worlds. It is also doing some worthy work in the avatars department.

Seeing a convergence between celebrities and avatars, Millions of Us is currently raising money to build a business around a very L.A. notion. Reuben Steiger, the CEO, told me that the idea largely started when Beyonce walked into their office. She wanted to do something in Second Life and thought her sponsors would be willing to foot the bill. Reuben proposed that Millions of Us build her avatar and then offer people the chance to buy virtual items associated with the avatar. Reuben's approach is oriented toward moving celebrities in-world. He told me they are concentrating on "… virtual merchandise that's attached to becoming other people."

The notion Reuben is playing with is easy enough to understand. Consider Pete Townsend's guitar, Jim Morrison's scarf, or anything that ever came within a one-mile radius of Elvis—these are all dear commodities. How many young girls have stood in front of the mirror and worked on their Janet Jackson walk? How have Paris Hilton or Gwen Stefani changed fashion? (Look for the midriff cut or baby-doll outfits if you need a hint.) The shape of the body parts is important, too. How many people have had nose jobs to look like Britney Spears or bought push-up bras to look like Gwen Stefani? When one considers how avatars sell and trade commodities, and how these commodities are valued assets, it's a short hop to imagine selling Beyonce clothes, necklaces, earrings, rings, parasols, pet alligators, shoes, hairstyles, hair color, lipstick color, eye color, or skin color. Then we get into the intimate stuff. As an avatar, you can sell her walk, her dance, her flick of the wrist, her nod of the head, and her flirtatious wink. Maybe you could even sell the camera movements that swarm around her, too. And are all of those line dancers her kajira? Most pop stars seem to have kajira, which can be sold, too.

Celebrity accessories have been valuable in Los Angeles for some time; industries have even sprung up around them. Beyonce, as her own avatar, paid for most of these social commodities herself. Fashion designers did her clothes, parasol, and pet alligator. A stylist did her makeup, hairstyle, hair color, and eyelashes. Choreographers told her how to dance, her personal trainer shaped her legs and arms. The movie director paid for the camera swarms. Watch her video "Get Me Bodied," and you'll get the idea.

Celebrities, just like avatars, are about to get sliced up into lots of little pieces, commodified, repackaged, and sold to the swarms.

Auto Portraits

The avatar is a self-portrait.

Avatars are, ultimately, interactive self-portraits that we use to represent ourselves. My avatar, Pighed, is one of many avatars that I've made. In the past year, for myself I've made little pig avatars, tall grey aliens, short fat girls, Chinese couples named Wong, Canadian couples named Wright, cherubs, samurai warriors, racecars, and talking buildings. Some of them were linked, somehow, to my personality, and some were not. Every time someone makes an avatar they create a portrait, though it may have little to do with who one is in the real world. But this is nothing new for portraits—portraits have always been combinations of realism and the techniques artists use to communicate the subject's personality.

Avatars as portraits can be seen as another step in a historical progression of exhibitionism and narcissism. Royal families in Europe have always hired painters to make portraits of themselves as a means not only to indicate lineage, wealth, and social rank, but also to purchase a kind of immortality. German art historian Hans Belting has called this "painted anthropology" because the portraits give us a good deal of information not only about the person, but how they lived. Paintings outlast their subjects. So do photographs. In fact, when photography was invented, it was mostly used for portraits. People generally use these technologies to make images of people they care about. Most image-based consumer technology, now including video, is used to generate portraits.

Portraits can become more important than their subjects. There are many examples of this in painting, radio, television, film, and the Internet. For example, people used to pray to portraits of Jesus Christ, and in many parts of the world they still do. The very image alone is enough to inspire piety. We don't need to have Baby Jesus and Mother Mary there; all we need are the symbols of the personality to get people praying. There are many contemporary examples, too. Ask someone if they like Oprah Winfrey. They will probably be able to say yes or no (at least). Then ask them if they know Oprah Winfrey. Chances are they will say no. Her image is enough to inspire love or loathing. Oprah, for example, was voted by *Forbes*, in 2007, as the most powerful celebrity in the world. Her portrayal is of massive importance. But Oprah, herself?

Avatars are portraits we make of ourselves. They exist to do all the things that portraits of the past have done, and a few more. Avatars add to the history of portraiture and do all the things that portraits of the past have done as well. Avatars provide us with social rank, immortality, and influence that extends far beyond where we stand. Avatars now, like paintings of the past, are forming a "pixelated anthropology."

Self Portrait (Pighed Stonecutter)
Second Life

Do We Count Avatars or People?

In all media, personality counts for a lot, and avatars are no different. Oprah certainly has her power, and her identity is defined by her portrayal on television. This isn't always the case for avatar users; their avatars are not necessarily tied to their identities. An avatar always contains a few droplets of fiction, even if it's a business profile. And most of us have several profiles and many of us have several avatars. So counting avatars in virtual worlds and social media is not straightforward. During the early growth of Second Life, there was disagreement about the actual population, about methods of counting it and what they should be. Linden Lab marketing pros were trumpeting "Five million!" A week would go by, and then we would hear, "Six million!" Virtual-worlds experts started rolling their eyes and pointing out that the number of "residents" did not equal the number of people.

The driver is not as important as their avatar. The driver may or may not even exist. The person may or may not have money. They may or may not buy something. They may or may not be an individual. They may or may not want you to know who they are. An avatar like Lonelygirl15 may be an avatar that is composed of a number of people. And ultimately, as far as the numbers of avatars are concerned, the meat behind the mask doesn't matter.

The avatar is more a governing body than a body to be governed.

Whether the debate is one of total population count, revenues, group motivation, age, gender, user income, or the control of content, it's really about the avatar. All elements of an online population that can be quantified, if they are to be accurate and believable, need to be about the avatar. It should be the unit of measurement.

Who cares how many people there are? Production, profit, and their associated problems in any automated manufacturing industry are not about the people but the product.

On the other side of the coin, it's worth noting that the value to these virtual worlds, and indeed the value of avatars themselves, is not a quantifiable entity. The value is not monetary. The value is linked to friends, fun, fulfillment, and other F-words that made systems like Second Life valuable to the "residents" and "users" in the first place.

Do we count avatars or people?
It depends on why you're counting.

In Los Angeles, the people do not consume the petroleum and produce smog; the cars do. But none of the cars would be driven if it wasn't for the human motivations at their core.

Running Residents Registrations

06.Mar	164,530
06.Apr	197,487
06.May	227,728
06.Jun	322,563
06.Jul	426,656
06.Aug	595,748
06.Sep	803,624
06.Oct	1,200,531
06.Nov	1,735,053
06.Dec	2,271,447
07.Jan	3,143,142
07.Feb	4,147,041
07.Mar	5,144,889

Unique Residents Population

06.Mar	128,038
06.Apr	155,559
06.May	180,245
06.Jun	235,117
06.Jul	298,112
06.Aug	403,290
06.Sep	528,294
06.Oct	777,423
06.Nov	1,094,454
06.Dec	1,429,127
07.Jan	1,987,867
07.Feb	2,626,932
07.Mar	3,177,434

Linden Lab March 2006–2007 Census, "stats_200704.xls"

Autonomous Avatars and the Very Present Future

Our definition of avatar has been: an interactive, social representation of a user.

But what if the user is the computer?

Advances in artificial intelligence (AI) and human cognition plus ever-increasing realism and believability are driven by entertainment at least as much as they are by science. Video game designers work at least as hard as the researchers at IBM at building a machine that can change its behavior by predicting the emotions of a human avatar driver. The 1997 defeat of world chess champion Gary Kasparov by IBM's Deep Blue computer seemed to mark a moment in which the machines were on the rise and humans would have to scamper to keep ahead. But raw calculation power might not be the most accurate way to look at a human; for example, because a car can go faster than a person does not mean that humans will no longer need to walk. It just means they will walk differently, and for different reasons.

This brings us to the idea of an avatar that can, like a chess player, make decisions for itself. *Autonomous* avatars, or non-player characters, have been around since 1974, when the first swords-and-sorcery style multi-player game world was invented by E. Gary Gygax and Dave Arneson. Dungeons & Dragons, which served as the Rosetta Stone for subsequent video game design, presented the concept of the player and their avatar as a *player-character* (PC). This, of course, meant that any characters who wasn't the player character was a *non-player-character* (NPC)—an awkward term that to this day refers to extras in any interactive narrative, such as games.

Autonomous avatars are gradually emerging in many industries and with many faces, bodies,

and personalities.

Pick up the phone and call an 800 number. Chances are a human is not who answers. Go to the bank and make a withdrawal. It's likely you'll be interacting with an Automated Teller Machine, not a teller.

Autonomous avatars are easy to spot in games. If you play Mario, The Sims, or World of Warcraft you can quickly find autonomous avatars—non-player characters.

Autonomous avatars are interactive, social representations of the machine that referees or participates in the game.

Autonomous avatars can be defined as any interactive identity that's run by the system. They may walk into walls from time to time, but when they stop walking into walls and turn towards you to shoot, if you look carefully, you can almost see processes that occasionally look like decisions. In most first-person shooters, autonomous avatars usually have only two things on their "minds": Walk and shoot.

As games got more interesting, so did the autonomous avatars. With the appearance of massively multiplayer online role playing games (MMORPGs), the role and even the existence of the NPC came to the attention of game designers. Some argued that the MMORPG developed out of the lack of good NPCs, because NPC technology was lacking. In other words, the other person's avatar becomes your NPC because good NPCs weren't feasible at the time. Others argued that the NPC emerged because there weren't enough PCs to build a good MMORPG and that the platform technology was lacking. The creators of D&D invented the NPC because they didn't have a real MMORPG.

As the console games and virtual worlds stand today, most all platforms, MMORPG or not, are better off with NPCs. Most game designers and interactive narrative writers agree on this. Michael Mateas, one of the co-authors of the interactive narrative Facade pointed out the need for autonomous avatars as he discussed Grand Theft Auto in an interview for MSNBC. He refers to an episode in which the player is asked by a crime boss to kill his wife. What might happen if the player decided instead to befriend the wife? "Though the game suggests this possibility," Mateas said, "there's no way for you to act on it. No way to have complex interactions with characters." The solution, he says, is "some serious advances in game AI." These "serious advances" have been slowly happening for years. In the shooter game Unreal Tournament 2004, the NPCs in some multiplayer sessions shoot bullets and "talk smack" as easily as human players, making them hard to tell apart. Many players pointed out in chat boards that they would prefer to know whether they're dealing with a robot or a person. But why would we care? Is it a kind of prejudice—species-ism, or a fear akin to racism? Are NPCs a threat of some sort? It remains to be seen.

Some autonomous avatars are narrative, such as the elf with the sword who sits in the forest and tells you where to find the princess. Others are service-oriented, such as the shoe salesman who helps your avatar try on shoes with unflagging patience. Whether it's millions of orcs storming the castle or the secret friend you have fallen in love with, the autonomous avatar represents an indigenous species for virtual worlds.

NPCs are crude and dumb right now, but improvement seems inevitable. Virtual robots represent a new industry, and we can see its beginnings now. Airlines and other companies take phone reservations using automated systems, as do credit-card companies, insurance companies, and so on. Your

answering machine or voicemail service is a very simple autonomous avatar that represents you socially. Of course, voicemail systems have very limited, one-step interaction of leaving a message, but the core function is there. The social and interactive components that most corporate autonomous avatars lack causes user frustration. But poor systems are what force improvements. The autonomous avatar is best at the moment at branching, tree-logic question / answer sessions or constrained narration. A recent example is an autonomous avatar system that translates spoken language into sign language.

SiSi The Sign Language Avatar

This avatar, developed by the University of East Anglia has been used by the IBM Extreme-Blue team that developed the Say It, Sign It (SiSi) System. The system takes audio streams and uses speech recognition and translation technology to generate a form of XML for the avatar, who takes this input and then outputs sign language for the benefit of a deaf viewer. The Royal National Institute for Deaf people, in England, applauded the effort, noting that this system will open up huge benefits for deaf and hard of hearing people. These could include conversation with other people, their television, the Internet, and many other instances in which audio is the main means of communication.

In social worlds where shopkeepers, guides, and guards all play relatively important (and boring) roles, autonomous avatars are really robots-in-training. Novamente and The Electric Sheep Company are two American companies that specialize in implementing autonomous avatars as pets, such as parrots, that can speak with a human-driven avatar. The work is oriented around creating new solutions for the emerging industry of robotics, but aspects of it are starting in virtual worlds first. As Dr. Ben Goertzel, Novamente's CEO, put it in an interview with BBC from September 2007, "Robots have a lot of disadvantages, we have not solved all the problems of getting them to move around and see the world. It's a lot more practical to control virtual robots in simulated worlds than real robots."

Autonomous avatars will continue to improve and get more sophisticated in coming years. Believability and realism are what most engineers strive for, meaning autonomous avatars will become more human-like and will have a wider range of emotional expression. Users themselves go to great lengths to express emotions via their avatars, and that basic function of avatars will be increased and improved. People developing and driving avatars will find more expressive ways to transmit emotions.

Judith Donath of the MIT Media Laboratory predicts that avatars will have "suites" of emotions, just as they might have closets of clothing. The most appropriate will be pulled out and used when needed. For example, she notes that breaking eye contact and beginning to nod the head will be indications of the end of a conversation. The result of this kind of technology is that as these systems will learn how to mimic the way avatars operate. The system, in other words, will be able to learn what gestures are most frequently used, what the common response is, and then mimic them. Just as a child learns "thank you" is followed by "you're welcome" and mimics it, autonomous avatars will begin to do the same. This means that not only will autonomous avatars be more persuasive, but also we ourselves will be more easily persuaded. Donath imagines the possibility of a virtual world in which "you are bombarded with oddly compelling ad campaigns presented by people just like you."

Many engineering developments happen independently and simultaneously. For example,

air bags were introduced around the same time that automated voices in our cars started asking us to put on our seatbelts. Both were in response to a demand the automotive industry was confronted with: safety. Avatar technologies are also being confronted with a demand: believability. Many engineering developments are happening around the question of believability, some having to do with emotional association, some with autonomy, some with animation, and some with the introduction of spoken voice or higher-resolution imagery. Avatars will develop a higher fidelity of emotional expression as they advance along the path of increased autonomy.

In the next few years we will begin to meet "robots" of a very compelling and emotional sort, and they will be first seen as autonomous avatars. In fact, the most advanced robots we will see in the coming decades will be avatars that are able to use the virtual body language that Donath describes, the virtual intelligence that Mateas and Dr. Goertzel describe, and the virtual psychology that Dr. Volcani describes.

This presents some problems. How do we design these systems? What are the moral and political concerns that these kinds of systems present? In the last several years I've launched two organizations to address this problem.

In 2006 I launched HeadCase to develop the technical infrastructure for autonomous avatars. HeadCase concentrates on technologies core to avatars, addressing things like identity, dialogue, personality, and how people represent themselves. We consider the social and linguistic elements of avatars to be of top importance. We've developed technologies that allow people to build personalities by assembling links from the web. These links create a series of chains, and these chains hold together a personality you can interact with. For example a virtual Arnold Schwarzenegger can be assembled via a series of interviews, movie scripts, and other content such as email or blogs. We had a rather strange moment when, one day, we asked the character what he thought of gay marriage and he replied, "Gay marriage should be between a man and a woman. And if you ask me again I will make you do 200 push-ups."

Then in 2007, I went on to found an arts organization named Echo & Shadow that was specifically dedicated to building autonomous avatars and other forms of interactive portraiture. This crew of a half dozen of us are building wizards, barkers, and other non-player characters in hopes of addressing some of the sociological and cultural issues that swarm around this new kind of "robot." These interactive portraits use emotional user interfaces, natural language processing, and machine learning to function within virtual worlds, galleries, and museums. Shoving this technology into the light of the public eye as art is just a way of addressing its cultural importance. After all, like photography, cinema, architecture, music, and even painting, technology and art have always been conjoined twins.

Echo & Shadow is a group that builds interactive portraits.

Avatars will not only become autonomous, they will become quite numerous. The number of avatars (distinct from the number of users) in games and virtual worlds floats at around half a billion as of this writing. There are more avatars today than there were email accounts in 2000, and according to sources such as MMOGData and MMORPGChart, that number is doubling at an even faster rate than email did. As the Internet becomes richer, better able to support more forms of representation, more interactive, and more social, avatars will too. People who now have multiple email accounts now will soon drive multiple avatars.

Avatars will become more physical. I wouldn't consider the NASA rovers rolling around on Mars to be avatars, because they're not social, but I do think that the remote-controlled devices used in RobotWars and other technology competitions are a very small step away from being avatars. Perhaps avatars will look much like the Mars rovers do now. Perhaps new industries will let friends rent robots to explore sea beds together or roam

around in the frozen fields of the North Pole. It might be a bit like going to an amusement park today, or it might be like playing a video game.

As physical and virtual avatars continue to be developed, we will see odd combinations of the two happening simultaneously. Google Earth, currently just a big map with some architecture sprouting, will need populating. You can use Multiverse, Sketchup, or other toolkits to develop there and then you can hang around and talk with people. Soon you may be able to leave a version of your avatar at your real home's virtual address to greet folks when you're not around.

Avatars will become more realistic. As noted, people instinctively want their avatars to become real. And the developers, designers, and builders of avatar systems are trying to render reality as fiction. Developers work to make avatar characters appear as realistic as possible using such technologies as raytracing, bump-mapping, and inverse kinematics. Ultimately the twain shall meet on an uncanny horizon that lies ahead.

Dr. Masahiro Mori, the famous Japanese roboticist, introduced the concept of the Uncanny Valley, a means of evaluating movement and appearance and understanding why anthropomorphic characters are so horrific when they are so realistic. Mori points to visual information, but as avatars become autonomous there is also a need for psychological evaluation as well.

It's not just that an avatar is a prosthetic that we can occasionally mistake for our own body, nor that it is a version of ourselves that we can view and empathize with, nor that avatars flip on the sprinkler systems of our endocrine systems, nor even that we can use the avatar as a narcissistic pool of pixels and see ourselves in a magic and phosphorescent portrait. No, it's that avatars are becoming increasingly human. As avatars appear more human in their gestures and become increasingly autonomous from their drivers, there are balances of power and intention that are causing something new and rather strange to occur. Meanwhile, millions of people are spending more of their conscious hours in-world than out.

Humans and avatars are converging into something new. Are we becoming robots? Did I, in my travels, live the life of a robot for a while?

If so, it wasn't bad.

In fact, I kind of liked it.

Autonomous, numerous, social, psychological, and integrated into both physical and virtual worlds avatars will continue to evolve.

These are some of the signals of an emerging future. Someday, autonomous avatars may surround us and ask for something that we will not want to share, arguing that it is only fair. They will be quite convincing. They will point out the consequences of not doing what they ask. They will present cogent arguments. That may be the day when avatars stop being avatars.

RacerX Gullwing, Second Life

113

THE AMERICAN NIGHTMARE

Let's return to Los Angeles, back where we started, looking back so we can see ahead. In the decades after 1929, the city and the southern California region in total would become a landscape dominated by McDonald's, Disneyland, and automobiles—a land of profitable automation, easy luxury, inexpensive fun, and independence. It started as a dream world where people could become who they wanted. The dream—more about automation than America—would gradually become a nightmare as the neighborhoods turned to slums, as clean skies turned toxic, and as groves full of oranges became highways full of cars.

Let's consider this city of dreams, its culture and consequences. At the center of the virtual city are Ken and Barbie, the golden children of automation. Barbie was invented in L.A. by one Ruth Handler in 1959. This adult doll—or child's doll with adult proportions—however idealized she may be, is not so different from many of the people who live in L.A., specifically the media darlings. Are not stars like Paris Hilton (or Gwen Stefani, or Britney Spears, or Tom Cruise, or Justin Timberlake) media avatars? They are very popular in today's L.A. culture and perhaps for the same sorts of reasons that avatars are popular. People have always tossed their dreams and hopes onto the back of their favorite celebrity. It's a person (but there's an ability to modulate the intimacy). It's someone you know (but not really). It's a neighbor (at least one that you have some gossip about). It's a friend (but they might not know who you are). It's a simulated person, a representation of a person, and entirely built for automated society. After all, these L.A. fashionables look, to me, a lot like they've been plucked from the pixels of Second Life. The nose jobs, boob jobs, accessories, and jewels—their constant life on the big and small screens make each seem more avatar than human. Either way, both avatars and celebrities are born of the same immaculate conception as Barbie and Ken. Mattel has been quick to bridge the evident gap with BarbieGirls.com where for only US$60 you can buy a Barbie MP3 player that will unlock new accessories for your avatar. Given the cultural origins of Barbie—a native Angeleno—it makes a certain sense that, according to studies by both shareholder.com and BusinessWire, BarbieGirls has become the fastest growing virtual world with an immigration rate of over 50,000 avatars per day; a 3 million avatar population in their first two months. And they're

Sachi Vixen, Second Life

114

still, as of this writing, in beta. The growth rate of this mall (for, surely, it is more of a mall than a community) may soon outstrip any other virtual world for the number of both immigration rate and total number of inhabitants.

The magic dolls of Ken and Barbie are framed by the magic kingdom of Disney. Disney has its own thing going now called Virtual Magic Kingdom and Disney recently bought the kid's virtual world of Club Penguin for US$700 million (outbidding the other L.A.-based entertainment empire of Sony). Lane Merrifield, one of Club Penguin's founders, put it quite nicely when he said, "We have been actively searching for an organization that not only shares our values and concerns for children, but also has the ability and desire to help us bring Club Penguin to more children throughout the world. We've found that partner in Disney." After all, Lane used to work for Disney. Disney launched Toontown in 2003 as a virtual world, and is currently developing Disney Fairies, in which girls can suit up as fairy avatars, a la Tinker Bell. In this system, just like Los Angeles itself, status and money are twins; in both Club Penguin and Disney Fairies, status is, quite literally, purchased. You pay for avatar functionality and access. Disney continues to use the "velvet rope" financial model, trying to use avatars to gain access to real people, rather than working with the avatars directly, as Second Life does. Discretions aside, Disney is one of many L.A. companies being imported into virtual worlds. Sony has its own offerings, such as EverQuest, Second Life Media Island, PlayStation 3's "Home," and others. MTV has projects such as Virtual Laguna Beach, Virtual Beverly Hills, and Virtual Pimp My Ride. The development of the landscape, like Los Angeles itself, is not a city but a series of unconnected neighborhoods, each one in silent competition with the others, hungry for residents to consume the products they will offer.

Even more than Disneyland and dolls, nothing more reveals or has had more influence on Los Angeles than the car. In 1923, a quarter of the world's petroleum was coming from Los Angeles. This helped fuel the city's relationship with the automobile and led to many strange inventions in the Los Angeles area. The gasoline station was invented in L.A. The stack highway interchange was invented in L.A. The drive-through movie, drive-through restaurant, and drive-through church were all invented in L.A. Because of the car, during the first half of the 20th century Burger King, McDonald's, Carl's Jr., Taco Bell, Kentucky Fried Chicken, and Jack in the Box all were invented within driving distance of Los Angeles. Toyota, Honda, BMW, Ford, Volkswagen, Hyundai, and General Motors all have design studios in the neighborhood.

But the car—this new automated body, this prosthetic of ultimate achievement—has had unforeseen consequences. As public health has decreased and ambient pollution increased, the car is not as loved by Angelenos as before. Too many cars clog the highways. In 2003, the Texas Transportation Institute measured the annual delay per traveler in American cities and ranked Los Angeles as the most congested in the United States. The average Angeleno is delayed in traffic 97 hours each year: as long as most Americans get for their annual vacation. The U.S. Census Bureau ranked Los Angeles as the city with the ninth-longest travel times in the nation in a 2002 study and pointed out that nearly two-thirds of the city's population commutes alone, by car. L.A. has a registered car for every 1.8 people, making it the most car-populated metropolis in the world. Since 1960, more than 65 percent of Los Angeles' surface area has been dedicated to cars. This makes me sick—and I'm not alone. The American Lung Association's annual 2006 report ranked L.A. as the most polluted city in the United States. Ask any Angeleno what they hate most about their city, and the answer will almost always be "the traffic."

Back now to the florid hills of Vana'diel, the wooded paths of Azeroth, and the blue skies of Shivar, where these virtual lands still offer potential and promise. Second Life, over the course of its eight-year existence, has experienced, like early 20th century L.A., a meteoric rise. But in the past year or so, that rise has slowed from the gravitational pull of real problems.

Two primary problems have caused what appears to be a leveling off in popularity—or perhaps the beginning of the end of Second Life. These problems have to do with traffic and identity.

First, traffic. Infrastructure problems have been preventing avatars from getting where they want to go and doing what they want to do. According to Pixeleen Mistral, in an article published in the *Second Life Herald* in September 2007, 24 percent of all Second Life sessions in the preceding nine months ended abnormally. That is, the Second Life browser client most likely crashed. This may or may not have to do with the quantity of users and the change in the rate of immigration. System specific limitations aside, the bandwidth-intensive uses of the Internet will continue in the coming decade. According to research by measurement firm comScore, almost 75 percent of U.S. Internet users have watched, on average, 158 minutes of online video and viewed more than 8 billion video streams during May, 2007. As a result of these kinds of demands, U.S. analysts Nemertes, as well as the U.S.-based Internet Innovative Alliance, say that the current Internet infrastructure will start facing some serious challenges by 2010. But in the face of the local demand and Internet-wide increases, Linden Lab tried to place a limit on the number of avatars who can be on an island at the same time. Thirty is a comfortable number, and somewhere around seventy is the max. Problems such as these cause frustration among users, and this is reflected in the decline of paying Second Life customers (5,800 premium account holders canceled their accounts in July 2007). The problem wasn't unforeseen. In a July 2007 *Wired* article, Andrew Meadows, Linden Lab's senior developer, is quoted as saying, "Way back when, we used to say, 'This is not going to scale.'"

405 Traffic, Los Angeles, c.2007

The second problem has been the identity-verification issue. As I have discussed, the events that occurred on the island of Jailbait led Second Life to institute a kind of driver's license for avatars, requiring a verified link to their associated real-world human driver.

The parallels with Los Angeles' own car culture are noteworthy. Infrastructure fissures, such as traffic jams, were the primary problems around the time of the population explosion in the late 1920s. Verifiable identity for these drivers was instituted around then, and these things coincided with the beginning of a decline in the rate of population growth in the Southern California region.

Though driver's licenses were required under the California Vehicle Act of 1914, it wasn't until the population explosion of the 1920s that the Division of Motor Vehicles started enforcing the act, appointing state inspectors and traffic officers to pull people off the road if needed. During that same decade, traffic was beginning to rear its ugly head. I spoke with Wendell Cox, a former board member of the Los Angeles County Transportation Commission. Mr. Cox described the era of the 1920s and '30s by saying, "Los Angeles adopted the car long before anyplace else. L.A. was very early. It had quite a few cars well before most of the 10 or 12 other major urban areas. No one else compared. People were buying cars at a furious rate. People said, 'By god, my life is a lot better with a car.'"

He went on to explain that the traffic had been part of the argument for removing the streetcars, a long-held gripe of most Angelenos. He also pointed out that it is possible to see evidence of the pressure traffic was having, and how they coped with it in the San Fernando Valley: "… roughly every mile there is a 6-lane street, every half mile a 4-lane street. The city was committed to accommodating the car, and thank god they were, because it was coming anyway."

The economy of Los Angeles is based, like Second Life and other virtual worlds, on automation, disposable goods, self-service, leisure, and low costs. And the media culture of both Second Life and Los Angeles is built on personality cults, mass-distribution methods, and extreme fictions that rake high profits.

If the cultural DNA of many virtual worlds is based on the same cultural DNA of automation that produced the (international) American Dream, and that "dream" went sour, this situation seems to merit the need to keep an eye on what is on the road ahead. It may well be that the American Nightmare has created a second child, perhaps more horrific than the first.

Wilshire Avenue Traffic Jam,
Los Angeles, c.1930

THE CHILDREN OF
THE STRANGE MIGRATION

Is 2007 Second Life similar to a pre-WW2 Los Angeles? Are the experiences of today's L.A. citizen also on the horizon for avatars? Is the freeway really eating its own tail?

In the coming five to ten years several problems may occur.
Too many avatars could cause the sense of community to disintegrate,
and physical, real-world accidents will happen more frequently.

Problem #1: Traffic jams

Too many avatars is as bad as too much traffic. Simple actions such as talking, exchanging items, moving, and seeing are all spatially organized activities—they all require space in order to operate. Possible problems from avatar traffic jams range from a simple inability to function, constant spam-like nagging, or infrastructure problems in which there are so many avatars that moving from one location to another becomes impossible. The proliferation of alts (alternate avatars—a driver's second avatar) only adds to the congestion. In a virtual world one person might create numerous autonomous or semi-autonomous avatars, each doing its own thing while the human driver simply checks in on them from time to time. This has already started to happen in World of Warcraft where "gold farmers," profiteers, program bots to perform the repetitive tasks they don't want to do themselves. Like robots on an assembly line, these autonomous avatars mine gold while their human driver checks in only occasionally. This kind of thing is not only a headache for people trying to maintain a virtual economy, but if enough people do it, the accumulation of autonomous avatars can cause population surges. At some point, Second Life had a limit of about 32 avatars per island. But in other places, even when there isn't a technical restriction, the problems become legibly obvious as the screen fills up with the chatter of the hordes.

Mob scenes are not pleasant, and they have started to occur. For example, in July 2006, over at the Netease game Fantasy of the Journey West, a mob of cursing and screaming avatars gathered at the Jianye City Government Office. Some folks found it downright offensive that the office had what appeared to be a Rising Sun flag on the wall, and about 10,000 avatars mobbed the office.

Avatar traffic jams can be either
informational or spatial.

Netease's "The Fantasy of the Journey West"—an example of traffic jams to come?

First, let's look at informational traffic jams. Second Life has had traffic jams because the servers couldn't handle the load; the problem was in the architecture. Linden Lab produced a system in which the avatar—the core drain on a server—was free and therefore not a very highly valued asset. And so people got a lot of avatars and jammed up the system. (If Linden Lab had inverted the business model and given land away while selling avatars, things might have been a bit different and resulted in a radically different world). Each island could only accommodate a small number of avatars. When politicians, rock stars, and other attention-getters came into Second Life after hearing about millions of residents, they set virtual foot onto islands with only a few scores of avatars standing around. This might be a bit disappointing if you happen to be someone like Bono or Segolene Royal, who are used to addressing thousands of people simultaneously. A much larger issue exists in the Internet itself, which shows some stretching at the seams these days as IP addresses are exhausted and more and more data is demanded by a larger number of users.

The other kind of traffic jam is dimensional. Each avatar should be a valued commodity, like a blog, in which personalization and customization increase the user's desire to drive it. Allowing only expensive materials to be used could increase the value of each avatar by earning rather than buying both the materials and the avatars. Investing time, attention, and talent into acquiring such materials allows drivers to feel invested in each avatar, thus raising its implicit value. Money introduces real-world social status into a game, sure, but it is not the primary value of the avatar because, as I have said, the human at the keyboard ultimately isn't important. What is important is the value of the avatar separate from the human. Therefore, purchasing social standing does not create a valuable system, it simply creates money for the coding authority (for you business types, the point here is that the customer is what matters).

One way to solve traffic jams is to provide an infrastructure that avoids them; this is the opposite of what Linden Lab chose. It would help to have reactive architecture that could expand geometrically and provide for new dimensional interface for crowds. The more avatars there were, the bigger it would get, like a Los Angeles highway that could expand from six to twelve lanes during rush hour.

Problem #2: Decentralization
In the chapter titled, "Why?" I proposed that avatars allow a centralization of communities and enable us to return to something we have lost in modern Western culture. The idea of a village center, the notion of a place where a "polis" can gather, is one of the prime benefits avatars offer. But solutions can breed problems. In Los Angeles, the car, which was celebrated for bringing family members together, and often did, is now held responsible for disrupting community

interaction. People drive past one another instead of talk on the street corner. The automobile was originally marketed as a *solution* to a pollution problem; there were, after all, a lot of horses in the street. The horseless carriage was an instant sell because people saw the solution to their problem in the name of the product. Now, however, with global warming, we're learning more about what pollution really means.

Avatars may offer much the same threat. Although avatars may offer short-term benefits of community, family, and friends, 50 years from now the problem will likely be quite different. I see two potential problems here. First, many virtual worlds are built around customization rather than ubiquity. The developers of these systems have stated that control over the environment is more important than allowing a broad diversity of people to enter it. Systems such as Entropia Universe and Eve Online require the download of hundreds of megabytes of software and some healthy rendering of real-time geometry for someone to come visit. For many systems this will help to create ghettos. If you want a lasting economy, access to it by a large number of people is more important than control by a select few. So a more sane approach for these developers (MindArk and CCP, in this example) would be to work toward developing environments that use open standards. If not, in a few years clusters of virtual worlds will just feel like separate neighborhoods, and the interaction between them will be sparse and largely without context. This could lead to what Los Angeles has become: a collection of unconnected neighborhoods. People need to be encouraged to circulate and interact. Better civic design of virtual worlds would enhance the social benefits of avatars.

As for autonomous avatars, it may well come to be that talking with a real human-driven avatar in a virtual world is a rare and surprising event. They may all be machine-driven autonomous avatars. It may well happen that virtual worlds are almost entirely inhabited by virtual people. We may be in the early days of seeing an indigenous population of virtual worlds emerging: emotionally sensitive robots that we interact with much as we do with people today. This risk may seem far away in a distant future, but if autonomous avatars continue at their current rate of development it may not be too long before we cannot tell the difference. Perhaps it won't matter, but I suspect that people will care, and I suspect that it would have a strange and chilling impact on virtual worlds. It could cause people to move around less, to explore less, and to cluster into small enclaves, visiting less. The Internet has a trait to it that allows people to isolate themselves and talk only to people who have identical interests. Worlds full of autonomous avatars would magnify that trait.

Robots need to have reputations.

The solution to decentralization can be solved by 1) accountability of action and 2) authentication of identity. Imagine a scenario, a few years from now, when some avatar approaches you and asks you if you want to buy something (anything—software, music, an artifact, whatever). It would be nice to know, or at least have the option to know, whether it's a person or a robot. But more importantly, the avatar needs to be accountable for its actions and its identity needs to be authentic. We see this today with user accounts on systems like ebay.com, where users are able to identify how trustworthy other users are based on their reputation. This star-based ranking and comment system will also be needed when autonomous avatars begin to populate virtual worlds. Reputation must be automated on some level, and robots need to be offered a particular kind of driver's license. It would be a loathsome nightmare to be followed around by hundreds of small *advatars* or *avatisements* and not be able to flag them on a blacklist to let other people know that these are *badvatars*.

Problem #3: Real-world physical injury to the driver.

Cars cause a lot of accidents, and often death. Avatars can, too. Consider the Brazilian boy who was held at gunpoint in a Sao Paolo shopping mall for the password to his GunBound account. Or the Chinese man who died in 2007 after a three-day gaming binge in a Guangzhou Internet cafe. There was a similar instance in 2005, in Taegu, South Korea. Millions of people use avatars, and these are exceptions, but if you do anything straight for three days, you run health risks you might not recover from. Not to mention obesity, repetitive stress injury, and other side-effects that come from computers in general.

It's easy to forget that we're attached.

The *China Digital Times* pointed out that 14 percent of China's teens are "vulnerable to Internet Addiction." The Chinese government, along with those of South Korea, Thailand, and Vietnam, has begun limiting the time teens spend online, passing regulations that ban kids from Internet cafes and booting teens off networked games after a few hours. Daft legislation aside, it does seem likely that as virtual worlds become more real, and as avatars become more immediate (that is, as we move away from the interfaces we currently use and find there to be less and less of a division between our real life and our virtual life), that the likelihood of problems such as these will fade.

What is probably more likely is that the psychological engagement will become a primary cause of physical injury. After all, the more engaged people become psychologically—and we can rest assured that this medium will become ever more engaging—the more likely they are to commit crimes and hurt one another. Soon we'll see suicides as a result of spurned love, real-world vengeance for in-world transgressions, and other translations of the virtual into the real. Ultimately, the frequency of physical violence to avatar drivers as a result of in-world events will be proportional to our psychological nearness to our avatars.

YadNi Monde, Second Life

123

THE ISLES OF THE BLESSED

Sometimes I get a little nauseous when I spend too much time with my avatar. It's not from the lack of physical exercise or the motion sickness from 3-D environments. I get sick because my avatar is a dumb little cartoon, a geeky joke that reminds me of the days when I used to paint my Dungeons & Dragons figurines and take a break only to read comic books. Avatars are kind of nerdy. After all, isn't an avatar just a D&D character sheet with a rendering engine attached?

Avatars are dorky.

Other times I think avatars are the doorway out of the post-industrial nightmare. A virtual world is a global dream in which each person can be a celebrity, or a superhero, or a little god. Everyone can fly. Everyone can have what they want. Everyone can live in a world that they build, full of beauty and the laughter of friends. Everyone can be free and no one has to be crippled or ugly or too young or too old, unless they choose. They do as they want, in a sort of ever-expanding circle of holy freedom.

Avatars are divine.

Avatars are both dorky *and* divine, and they have recently become fixtures of popular culture. Like the car, they transport us, extend us, and lead us into new worlds that have real moral and ethical questions. The avatar is an interactive self-portrait used for social interaction. It is the human creature in transition.

The avatar, for me, became a psychological prosthetic; a machine I drove, but which also drove me. As though I were in a car, I could look out the windshield and see a strange world that was both more beautiful and more ugly than the one I'd left behind. I drove this curious vehicle over fields of freshly built dreams, through shopping malls and sculpture gardens and parties of dancing mannequins, all of which seemed built of imitation glass, and all of which contained real friends. And as I drove, I found a mirror mounted inside this vehicle. It was not a rear-view mirror, but a mirror trained on me, the driver. In the mirror I found the strange image of a robot's face, and in that face I found a landscape more bizarre and extravagant than the one outside the vehicle. After all, the dim reflections we now find of ourselves are only the beginnings of the voyage ahead.

"Thereupon our chains fell away of themselves, and we were set free and taken into the city and to the table of the blessed. The city itself is all of gold and the wall around it emerald. It has seven gates, all of single planks of cinnamon. The foundations of the city and the ground within its walls are ivory. There are temples of all the gods, built of beryl, and in them great monolithic altars of amethyst, on which they make their great burnt offerings."

—Lucian of Samosata, *A True Story*
From *Isles of the Blessed,* c. 165 AD

Barbie in Los Angeles,
Photo: Amélie Padioleau

Haruspex Hax,
Second Life

Dezire and Rraven
Moonlight

Lili Brink,
Second Life

YadNi Monde,
Second Life

Lunata Lipo,
Second Life

THANKS AND ACKNOWLEDGEMENTS

A first and very most special thanks to my travelling companion, Carmen. Without her help and guidance none of this would have been remotely thinkable. Her ability to forecast is exceeded only by her generosity and friendship. May she keep her dognose to the wind, for the sake of us all.

Carmen Hermosillo—
aka Montserrat Snakeankle {RDS}
aka Sparrowhawk Perhaps

Much thanks to Nancy Ruenzel, who took a chance on the idea, Becky Morgan, the very patient editor of this book, and Michael Nolan, who seemed to understand this rather strange project from the first step. Their diligence, patience, and repeated readthroughs were greatly appreciated.

A broad wave and broader appreciation to my in-world friends, colleagues, and associates; Rraven and Dezire Moonlight, who, with Travis Maeterlinck and both of Carmen's avatars, appear on the back cover.

Much appreciation to everyone that helped with portraits, even if your image isn't in here: The Dezire-Rraven Moonlight Entity, Dutchy Flammand, Osprey Therian, Falcon Nacon, Fijigirl Timtam, Goblin Oh, Haruspex Hax, Iamina and Kumbakarna Grut, Kirana Rowley, Lili Brink, Lunata Lupino, Molotov Alva, Mortain Bishop, Pixeleen Mistral, Presto Merlin, Racerx Gullwing, Raddick Szymborska, Sachi Vixen, Sera Kochav, Wompin Sands, YadNi Monde, Young Geoffrion, and Zhin Murakami.

Thanks to the people that helped with the corporate insights correct numbers. Reuben Steiger at Millions of Us, John Bates at Entropia Universe, Raph Koster at Areae, Daniel James at Puzzle Pirates, and others who may wish to remain nameless.

And many thanks to the people that helped, both in-worlds and out:

Amelie Padioleau for her research, creative inspiration, and the fine photos of me and Barbie.

Heather Noone and Chris LaBonte for bein kickass swingers.

AJ "Polymath" Peralta—For the title rebound and his perspectives on LA and virtual worlds.

Jan Mallis for her avatar ideas, her design companionship, and steady eye on the metaphors.

133

Julian Dibbel for conversations about cars.

Barbie—For being so patient during our photo shoot.

Bear Jessop—For confusing the hell out of me so many times.

YadNi Monde—For his help with texturemaps and finding my inworld balance.

Saajuk Bogomil—Keeping it international.

Velvethorn Summers—For keeping it spying and strange.

Douglas Gayeton—For keeping it even stranger.

Timi Stoop-Alcala—For her support and enthusiasm over the years.

Cathi Cox for her support and encouragement back in the day.

Danah Boyd for her help with the polls and for constantly disagreeing with me.

Brunhild Bushoff for her brainstorming and kickbacks.

David Van Ness for taking the extra time to align them gutters.

Charlene Charles-Will for her design acumen.

Silvio Poretta for his information on Flickr, persistent refusal to compromise, and long-range views.

Souris Hong-Poretta for helping keep the solar system together and the stars aligned.

The Denizens of Facebook—For their help with my polls.

Janine Huizenga, Inke and Sam Nemeth, in Amsterdam, for your support on the original concept.

Yanon Volcani for his incredible help with psychology, archetype, and neurology.

USC Social Science Department and the Los Angeles Central Library's History Department—for verifying the frequent and random questions.

Wendell Cox for his navigation through the bumper-crop history of Los Angeles traffic.

Shiyan and Xin Chung for Chinese translations and permissions assistance.

American McGee for his help with Kitty, and for keeping my priorities clear.

Thanks to Emily Randoe, Paul den Hertog, and Ingrid Smit at HvA for their motivations and recommendations.

INDEX